SELECTIONS FROM
HOCCLEVE

SELECTIONS FROM
HOCCLEVE

EDITED BY
M.C. SEYMOUR

CLARENDON PRESS · OXFORD

1981

Oxford University Press, Walton Street, Oxford OX2 6DP

London Glasgow New York Toronto
Delhi Bombay Calcutta Madras Karachi
Kuala Lumpur Singapore Hong Kong Tokyo
Nairobi Dar es Salaam Cape Town
Melbourne Auckland

and associate companies in
Beirut Berlin Ibadan Mexico City

Published in the United States by
Oxford University Press, New York

British Library Cataloguing in Publication Data
Hoccleve, Thomas
Selections from Hoccleve,
I. Title   II. Seymour, M.C.
821'.2   PR2091.5   80–42193
ISBN 0-19-871083-6
ISBN 0-19-871084-4 Pbk

Typesetting by Hope Services, Abingdon
and printed in Great Britain
at the University Press, Oxford
by Eric Buckley
Printer to the University

IN MEMORIAM

GABRIEL M. LIEGEY

PREFACE

Since the completion of this book in 1968 for the now defunct New Clarendon Medieval and Tudor Series, several scholars have written on Hoccleve, and in revising my text for this publication I have taken the opportunity to refer to their work. To them and their predecessors, especially F.J. Furnivall and E.P. Hammond, I owe much.

Bodley's Librarian and the custodians of the British Library, the Henry E. Huntington Library, University of Durham Library, and Yale University Library have kindly given permission to print from manuscripts in their care.

I am very much indebted to the Delegates for accepting this book for publication out of series and to their advisers and officers for their very kind help and guidance.

The Feast of St. Elizabeth,   M.C.S.
1980

CONTENTS

INTRODUCTION

Life

The official records, mainly Chancery rolls, cite Hoccleve on numerous occasions, from a time shortly before 21 June 1387 to a posthumous notice on 8 May 1426.[1] In addition, Hoccleve gives much personal detail in his poetry.[2] From these records and references it is possible to discern the main outlines of a biography in more certain detail than is usually available for late medieval English writers.

Born about 1368, Hoccleve entered the office of the Privy Seal[3] at Easter 1387 at the age of 19, living at the Keeper's *hospicium* then at Chester's Inn in the Strand and working at Westminster. His name, and possibly his person, perhaps derived from the village of Hockliffe, Bedfordshire, and he probably owed his appointment to patronage, perhaps of Guy de Rouclif, then a senior clerk in the Privy Seal, but nothing is known. The salary of the Privy Seal clerks (at 7½*d* a day) was paid out of the Keeper's daily allowance of twenty shillings until 1399, when a system of annuities was adopted instead; there were seven, perhaps eight, clerks of the Privy Seal at this

---

[1] Most of the records are printed by F.J. Furnivall, *Hoccleve's Works The Minor Poems*, EETS, e.s. lxi (1892, revised 1970), pp.li-lxx with the addition of seven further references on pp.lxxi-ii by the revisers. References to other records of Hoccleve's life are given by Brown, Green, Ingram (cited below).

[2] Every personal reference by Hoccleve in his verse that can be corroborated by other evidence is trustworthy. No doubt some of these carry a deliberate artistic emphasis (e.g. his statements of near-penury), and others of an impersonal nature (e.g. his claim that he wrote the *Tale of Jonathas* for the anxious father of a wild youth) are poetic fictions, yet the essential historical veracity of his references to himself is beyond question and explained by the nature of his verse, poems for public occasions for one or more persons who knew him well.

[3] The most informative account of Hoccleve's life at the Privy Seal is A.L. Brown, 'The Privy Seal Clerks in the Early Fifteenth Century', *The Study of Medieval Records . . .* (1971), ed. D.A. Bullough and R.L. Storey, pp.260-81. Cf. H.S. Bennett, *Six Medieval Men and Women* (1955), pp.69-99, and A.C. Reeves, 'Thomas Hoccleve, Bureaucrat', *Medievalia et Humanistica*, n.s. 5 (1974) 201-14. See also T.F. Tout, *Chapters in the Administrative History of England* v (1930), and 'Literature and learning in the English Civil Service in the fourteenth century', *Speculum* 4 (1929) 365-89.

time. In addition, each clerk was lodged and fed in the Keeper's household, given an annual Christmas gift of four ells of coloured cloth for robes, and might expect occasional perquisites like the grant of a corrody, a share in forfeited goods, a secular office or benefice, as well as fees and favours from those who used his services as an official of the government. For a time Hoccleve served as underclerk to Guy de Rouclif (d. after 3 December 1392) before the latter became Master of the Mint; Rouclif had dealings with Gower and bequeathed Hoccleve a copy of *De bello Troie*.[4] On 22 January 1394 Hoccleve was granted a corrody at Hayling priory, which he must have commuted to cash. On 3 September 1398 he was one of four Privy Seal clerks who shared a forfeit of £40.[5] On 12 November 1399 he received from the newly crowned Henry IV an annuity of £10, payable at Easter and Michaelmas until such time as he should be preferred to a living worth £20 a year; the qualification was common, not particular to Hoccleve. In 1401 he shared with seven others in the Privy Seal a special payment of £40.[6] Also about this time he cooperated in writing a manuscript of Gower's *Confessio Amantis*, presumably for money.[7]

During these early years of manhood, while probably in minor orders and waiting for a benefice, Hoccleve began to write verse, as he says, with Chaucer's encouragement. None of his extant work can be certainly dated to this time, but it is probable that much of his religious verse was written then. His first dated work, the *Letter of Cupid*, a modified translation made in 1402 of Christine de Pisan's *L'epistre au dieu d'amours* of 1399, marks a turning towards secular verse, and in the first decade of the fifteenth century he wrote a number of light-hearted occasional pieces. The most important of these, *La Male Regle de T. Hoccleve*, shows him (somewhat tongue-in-cheek) leading an expensively convivial and mildly foolish life in his leisure hours. Though doubtless some of this self-exposure is accurate in its detail, much of the comic

---

[4]   E.M. Ingram, 'Thomas Hoccleve and Guy de Rouclif', *Notes and Queries* 20 (1973) 42-3. J.H. Fisher, *John Gower* . . . (1964), pp.62, 339.
[5]   Brown, p.268.
[6]   Ibid., p.267. The payment was an extraordinary reward for past service.
[7]   A.I. Doyle and M.B. Parkes, 'The production of copies . . .' in *Medieval Scribes, Manuscripts and Libraries* . . . (1978), ed. M.B. Parkes and A.G. Watson, pp.198-9.

emphasis is due to Chaucer's example. The friends and patrons among the aristocracy and administrators whom his verse attests during these early years were those of a rising young man. His verse-making did not interfere with his official duties. He was given an under-clerk, John Welde, before 1408, and on 17 May 1409 (retrospective to the previous Michaelmas) his annuity was increased to twenty marks (£13.6s.8d.). Perhaps as a cause or effect of this new annuity, which no longer carried the king's qualified promise of a benefice, he married and removed from the *hospicium* of Chester's Inn to a *pore cote* nearby. During this period of sober industry and light-hearted verse he developed or maintained a diligent interest in books, in contemporary vernacular works like the *Canterbury Tales* and *L'epistre au dieu d'amours* as well as Latin histories like *De bello Troie*, which finds expression in his later work.

In 1411 he completed his major work, the *Regiment of Princes*, which he addressed to Prince Henry. Such an address on such matters, the virtues necessary to a ruler, was not as presumptuous as it might appear; Henry was already bookish and already very interested in Aegidius de Columna (one of Hoccleve's sources), and there were precedents for presenting him with compositions.[8] No doubt as a result of the favour which the *Regiment* attained, Hoccleve became on Henry's accession on 21 March 1413 an acknowledged quasi-official writer of verse on political occasions. The most important of several poems of this type that can be dated to this period was the *Remonstrance against Oldcastle*, written in August 1415.

The prospect of royal preferment which thus opened before Hoccleve was partly blighted by the death of Edward, duke of York (to whom he had sent a copy of the *Regiment*) at Agincourt in 1415, and then wholly shattered by a severe mental disorder, which had afflicted him by 8 July 1416. Although he had recovered his wits and resumed his work at the Privy Seal by 1 November 1416, his credibility and his confidence were destroyed. By the time that he was ready to take up his verse again in November 1421, Henry V was in France and soon to die, and another poet, Lydgate, was establishing himself by sheer volume as the dominant voice in English letters.

Hoccleve's poetic mood had, in any case, changed. Introspective, aware of failing health and of the disappearance of

[8] E.F. Jacob, *Henry V and the Invasion of France* (1947), pp.30-7.

his hopes (made the more obvious by the successes of his former colleague John Frye, who entered the Privy Seal with him and became its Secondary),[9] he returned to the religious and moral concerns of his earlier verse. In a sequence of poems written for Duke Humphrey, *custos Anglie* in Henry V's absence in 1422, Hoccleve combined a personal *planctus* and justification with translations of two moral tales from the *Gesta Romanorum* and of Henry de Suso's *Ars sciendi mori.* It was a brave recovery, of poetic faith as well as personal competence, and it was probably at the Duke's urging that the Regent Council granted him a corrody tenable at the priory of Southwick, Hants on 4 July 1424, which he must have commuted to cash. In 1423 he was paid two marks for writing to the Council on behalf of the Earl Marshal and for writing and sealing the subsequent warrant.[10] He received the last recorded payment of his annuity on 11 February 1426 and died at the age of 58, while still a clerk at the Privy Seal where he served for forty years under four kings, before 8 May 1426.[11]

Poems

The canon of Hoccleve's poetry is firmly established, and many of his poems can be firmly dated. His minor poems and the 'sequence' for Duke Humphrey (except its first quire) exist in holograph, and the *Regiment of Princes* is full of personal reference. Outside this canon lie a number of fifteenth-century poems (the most important of which are the fourteen poems embedded in the prose translation of Deguileville's *Pèlerinage de l'âme* made in 1413) which have been attributed to him on various grounds. Apart from the Deguileville poems, none of these attributions is convincing.[12] At the

---

[9] Brown, pp.272-3.

[10] Ibid., p.269, citing *Bulletin of the Institute of Historical Research* xxvii (1954) 196.

[11] Ibid., p.270, where the reference to Hoccleve's retirement (for which there is no evidence) is due to a misunderstanding of the roll's *nuper*: Furnivall, p.lxix. R.F. Green, 'Three Fifteenth-Century Notes', *English Language Notes* 14 (1976) 14.

[12] The following associations of single poems with Hoccleve are rejected on grounds of language, rhyme, metre, or bibliography: *Heyle be glad* suggested by H.N. MacCracken, 'Another poem by Hoccleve?', *JEGP* viii (1909) 260-6; three rhyme royal verses in a copy of the *Regiment* printed by R.H. Robbins, *Secular Lyrics of the XIVth and XVth centuries* (1952), pp.87, 93.

The fourteen Deguileville poems, printed by F.J. Furnivall, *Hoccleve's Regiment of Princes and 14 Poems*, EETS e.s. lxxii (1897) xxiii–lxii,

same time it is unlikely that all his minor poems have survived.[13] Though the categorizing of medieval poems can never be neatly precise, Hoccleve's verse does offer some scope for convenient description as religious verse (all undated and mostly early work), social verse (between 1402 and 1410), political verse (between 1411 and 1416), and the poems written for Duke Humphrey (in 1421 and 1422). His total output was approximately 13,000 lines — less than one-tenth of Lydgate's production — of which the *Regiment* constitutes over 5,500 lines.

Hoccleve's eleven religious poems, which vary in length from twenty-one to two hundred and forty-five lines, total 1,260 lines, less than one-tenth of his output. With two exceptions in eight-lined stanza rhyming *ababbcbc*, they are written in rhyme royal. Five of these poems are addresses to the Blessed Virgin, and three more concern legends associated with her. None can be dated, but three were written on request, the *Complaint of the Virgin* (245 lines) for Joan FitzAlan, countess of Hereford (d. 1419), three stanzas to the Blessed Virgin for Thomas Marleburgh, a London stationer (d. 1429), and a *balade* to the Blessed Virgin (160 lines) for Robert

include the *Complaint of the Virgin* which, without its initial stanzas, occurs in Hoccleve's holograph in the larger of the two manuscripts of his minor verse, Huntington Library MS HM 111. Six of them (excluding the *Complaint*) recur in a Carthusian miscellany, B.L. MS Additional 37049; see also P.D. Roberts, 'Some unpublished Middle English lyrics and stanzas in a Victoria Public Library manuscript', *English Studies* 54 (1973) 105-18. Whether the translator of the prose *Pèlerinage de l'âme* in 1413 appropriated more than one poem of Hoccleve is uncertain. On grounds of language, rhyme, metre, and bibliography there is a strong case for Hoccleve's authorship of them all, as Furnivall urged. However, the use of another's poems in such a context can be paralleled; e.g. Lydgate planned to use Chaucer's *ABC to the Virgin* in his verse translation of the *Pèlerinage de la vie humaine*; and Hoccleve's authorship is disputed by H.N. MacCracken in *The Nation* 85 (1907) 280-1, and by J.H. Kern, 'Een en ander over Thomas Hoccleve en zijn werken', *Verslagen en Mededeelingen der Koninklijke Akademie van Wetenschappen* 5 (1915) 336-90. The problem is examined by J. Smalley, 'Poems of the Middle English *Pilgrimage of the Soul*' (Liverpool M.A. thesis, 1953), who does not reach a conclusion. It may be that Hoccleve wrote the fourteen poems and translated the whole work for Joan FitzAlan, countess of Hereford, the maternal grandmother of Henry V, in 1413.
   [13] MS HM 111 certainly lacks initial leaves, perhaps quires, and the absence of poems on the victory at Agincourt, the death of Henry V, and his internment at Westminster, is unexpected.

Chichele (d. 1439), Master of the Grocers' Company, mayor of London in 1411–21, and brother of Archbishop Chichele (d. 1443). At least three of the religious poems (the *Complaint*, the *Balade*, and the story of the Virgin's sleeves) are translations from French. All these poems are competent exercises in poetic devotion but not otherwise distinguished, and they belong, most credibly, to Hoccleve's early attempts to find his voice.

This voice becomes more individual in the seven social poems written for the entertainment of friends and acquaintances and totalling 1,160 lines. All but two, the *Letter of Cupid* and *La Male Regle de T. Hoccleve*, are slight *jeux d'esprit* which generally revolve, in eight-lines stanzas, about *coynes scarsetee* and may be dated between 1407 and 1410. Two are addressed to Henry Somer before his promotion to Chancellor of the Exchequer in 1410, and a third, addressed more soberly to *my lord the Chanceller*, was also perhaps written to him. The other *jeux d'esprit* are a *balade* on a kindred theme to Master Carpenter, later town clerk of London (d. 1441) and three roundels. Both the *Letter of Cupid* and *La Male Regle* are more ambitious compositions. The former (476 lines in rhyme royal, written in 1402) is Hoccleve's only attempt at courtly and fashionable verse, based on Christine de Pisan's poem of 1399 and so immediately topical, and, exceptionally among Hoccleve's minor poems, seems to have circulated with modest success.[14] The latter (448 lines in eight-lined stanzas, written in 1405) is an original account of his bachelor vanities in London, humorously told under the guise of an apostrophe to Health and ending, characteristically, with an appeal to Thomas Nevil, the sub-treasurer, for payment of his annuity. Though the total number of lines in these social verses is even less than that in the religious verses, their impact is greater. They speak freshly to their matter, and in their carefree presentation of the poet's *persona* they make intelligible the development of Hoccleve's major work.

The poet's *persona* is fully developed in the long introduction to the *Regiment of Princes* (5439 lines in rhyme royal, written in 1411) which marks a major redirection of Hoccleve's verse towards political matters, though in intention it was also a major bid for royal favour and so a continuation of his

---

[14]   P.G.C. Campbell, 'Christine de Pisan en Angleterre', *Revue de littérature comparée* v (1925) 659–70. J.V. Fleming, 'Hoccleve's *Letter of Cupid* . . .', *Medium Ævum* 40 (1971) 21–40. The work survives in 10 manuscripts.

earlier laments of *coynes scarsetee.* The introduction (2016 lines and two-fifths of the whole), where Hoccleve in sober and sometimes despairing mood is advised by an Old Man, combines various literary *topoi* with an immediate personal application, and leads to a rehearsal of the fourteen virtues necessary to a ruler. Much of the substance of this is taken from three well-known medieval manuals on kingship (the pseudo-Aristotelian *Secreta Secretorum*; Aegidius de Columna, *De regimine principum*: Jacobus de Cessolis, *De ludo scaccorum*) which are worked with topical reference into an easily read and unified compilation, much regarded in the troubled years that followed Henry V's death in 1422. Its immediate acceptance may be seen in the political poems which Hoccleve wrote after Henry's accession in 1413, when four short *balades* (totalling 152 lines in eight-lined stanzas) commemorate his accession, the homage of his lords, the translation of Richard II's bones, and the holding of the chapter of the Garter knights. These are followed in 1415 by Hoccleve's major political verse, the *Remonstrance against Oldcastle* (512 lines in eight-lined stanzas), the most directly topical poem that Hoccleve wrote and (if one excepts a brief address to Henry after Agincourt for reimbursement of expenses) the last poem of these years. The tone of all this verse is that of a good servant confident that Henry V will be his good lord, and, with the obvious exception of the *Remonstrance*, the poems pleasantly complement the good-natured lightness of his social verse.

The mental illness that afflicted Hoccleve in 1416 left him without inclination to write, and when he eventually returned to his verse in 1421, it was in an introspective and melancholy mood. The sequence of poems written for Duke Humphrey in 1421 and 1422 is a compilation of five parts (3,829 lines in rhyme royal). The first two parts, the *Complaint* (413 lines) and the *Dialogue with a Friend* (826 lines), provide an autobiographical introduction (as in the *Regiment*) from which the other parts (two tales from the *Gesta Romanorum*, and Henry de Suso's poem on mortality[15]) proceed. They make a strange but not, in their context, incongruous compilation, which is thoroughly characteristic of Hoccleve in all

[15] Henry de Suso, *Horologium sapientie* ii.2. See B.P. Kurtz, 'The source of Occleve's *Lerne to Dye*', *Modern Language Notes* xxxviii (1923) 337–40, and 'The relation of Occleve's *Lerne to Dye* to its source', *Publication of the Modern Language Association of America* xl (1925) 252–75.

his poetic moods and which attained a modest deserved success.

Verse-forms and metre

Hoccleve had an essentially stanzaic concept of the structure of verse, eschewing both the four-stress and the Chaucerian five-stress couplets. This deliberate choice no doubt reflects a critical awareness of his own talents and subject-matter as well as of the advantages of the stanza: a generally self-contained rhetorical unit, easily built into a larger poem and so suited to fluent composition, and capable of accommodating Hoccleve's eclectic methods of translation and narrative. It is interesting to note, in view of his declared dependence on Chaucer, that this cautious, perhaps conservative, preference for the stanza as a verse form contrasts with its rejection by Gower and the later Chaucer. Hoccleve's literary ambitions, of course, were very much smaller than those of these greater poets (indeed, his poems were almost always designed with a view to preferment), and his choice of the stanza tacitly acknowledges that he has less complex and novel things to say than they have. At the same time his preference for the longer stanzaic forms, rather than the quatrain, indicates his desire for a rhetorical and dignified expression.

The bulk of his verse (the *Letter of Cupid*, the *Regiment*, and the 'sequence') is in rhyme royal, established by Chaucer's example in the *Troilus* as the most admired English narrative stanza. Most of the minor verse, however, is written in the heavier, more conservative eight-lined *balade* stanza (e.g. *Modir of Lyf*, *La Male Regle*, the *Remonstrance*), and the two surviving *envois* to the *Regiment* are in a nine-lined stanza, no doubt for contrast and emphatic conclusion. This critical distinction between rhyme royal and *balade* is not in itself a sign of sophisticated interest in form, but Hoccleve's occasional use of the *rondeau* and the *virelai* (see below, pp. 112, 125, 128) alongside the *balade* shows that he was aware of contemporary practice. In all these forms in English verse Chaucer was his precursor and very probably his mentor, as he claims in the *Regiment* 2078–9, and although his sources and references show that he was conversant with French and English forms beyond Chaucer's example, Hoccleve never ventured beyond his master into experiment. The existing stanzaic patterns were for him sufficiently varied to give him some scope in which to exercise his own judgement on the suitability of form to matter, and in none of his verse is that judgement noticeably suspect.

In the longer poems, that is those which exceed a few stanzas, Hoccleve worked at first within a general compass of 500 lines, more or less: e.g. *La Male Regle* 448, the *Remonstrance* 512, the *Letter of Cupid* 476, the *Complaint* 413, and much of the *Regiment* after the Prologue is built up of even smaller units; whereas Chaucer, for example, had a preferred length of about 700 lines for much of the *Canterbury Tales*. Within the 'sequence' Hoccleve extended his range somewhat: e.g. the *Dialogue* has 826 lines, *Jereslaus* 952, *Lerne to Dye* 917, *Jonathas* 672; and the difference may be due to a greater confidence, though the length of the last three of these poems is also partly due to the length of Hoccleve's sources. While the point need not be laboured, it does appear that as Hoccleve preferred the stanzaic structure, so he also preferred the equally self-contained 'short' poem.

Within these stanzaic patterns and units Hoccleve's metre is generally the five-stress line. With the conventional statement of modesty of a medieval poet (a *topos* also used by Chaucer) he confesses to *meetrynge amis* (the *balade* to the duke of York 48), and the phrase has helped to point much adverse criticism of his rhythms and, in particular, of his 'thwarted stress'. Such criticism depends upon an untenable belief in a regular English iambic line which evolved, as one might expect, in the eighteenth century without regard to the evidence of scribal punctuation and of textual transmission.[16] Yet many fifteenth-century manuscripts divide the five-stress line into two 'pauses' by using virgule or solidus and final point,[17] and this 'pausing' of the line allows the rhythms of natural speech (and much of such verse is in direct speech, while all of it is intended for recitation) to express themselves in an orally responsive metrical pattern. Thus, the opening stanzas of the *Regiment* allow the speaker to achieve a natural cadence without stumbling or affectation:

[16] Modern studies are J.G. Southworth, *Verses of Cadence* ... (1954) and *The Prosody of Chaucer and His Followers* ... (1962), and I. Robinson, *Chaucer's Prosody* ... (1971), C.S. Lewis in *Essays and Studies* 24 (1938) 28–41, E.P. Hammond, *English Verse between Chaucer and Surrey* (1927), pp.83–5, and F. Pyle, 'Chaucer's Prosody', *Medium Ævum* 42 (1973) 47–56.

[17] The manuscript evidence is neither uniform nor free from error, but in carefully prepared copies (such as the Ellesmere MS of the *Canterbury Tales* and Hoccleve's holographs) the patterns of punctuation are unambiguous.

Musynge / vpon the restlees bysynesse
Whyche that thys troubly world haþ ay on honde
That oþer thyng than fruyt of bytirnesse
Ne ȝyldeth nouȝt / as I can vnderstonde
At Chestres Yn / ryȝt fast by the Stronde
As I lay in my bedde / vpon a nyȝt
Thogȝt me berefte / of slepe the force and myȝt

The punctuation here, lacking in MS Arundel 38, is editorial. These lines are not extant in Hoccleve's holograph but, as with other scribal copies of his verse which have been metrically analysed,[18] the minor scribal disturbance of his forms does not affect the stressing which carries the rhythm. The same rhythmic fluency can readily be found in his holograph poems:

Of loues aart / yit touchid I no deel
I cowde nat / and eek it was no neede
Had I a kus / I was content ful weel
Bettre than I wolde han be with the deede
Theron can I but smal / it is no dreede
Whan þat men speke of it in my presence
For shame I wexe as reed as is the gleede
Now wole I torne ageyn to my sentence

In these lines from *La Male Regle* 153–60 Hoccleve has marked only those line divisions where such punctuation is needed to direct the pausing and so the stressing and fluency of the reader, and this is his general practice.

The last line of this quotation is apparently borrowed from the *Nun's Priest's Tale* 394, and is one of many similar direct echoes which illustrate the close influence of Chaucer's control of the line on Hoccleve's verse. This influence is particularly evident in Hoccleve's use of the pause to control the line, and more generally in his success, albeit within a much narrower emotive and narrative range, in telling a plain tale without subtlety and in discussing and reflecting on his hopes and fears. In such poems the balanced line, linked by rhyme within a simple stanzaic pattern and carrying the natural stresses of normal speech, moves forward rhythmically and unobtrusively, and its general syllabic length (pentameter with minor variation) comprehends a larger speech unit which sometimes overruns the end-stop. It is, in brief, a technically simple metre which is suited to Hoccleve's serious and reflective purposes because its rhythms are already present in ordinary English speech.

[18] Southworth, *Verses of Cadence*, pp.71–8; Robinson, pp.190–9.

This technical accomplishment sometimes falters when Hoccleve strives for more rhetorical effects, often by apostrophe and inverted word-order and more ambitious imitation of Chaucer's metrical subtlety, and when his invention resorts to padding before the demands of rhyme and length of line:

> Lond / rente / cattel / gold / honour / richesse
> þat for a tyme lent been to been ouris
> Forgo we shole / sonner than we gesse
> Palesses / Maners / Castels grete and touris
> Shal vs bireft be / by deeth þat ful sour is
> Shee is the rogh besom / which shal vs all
> Sweepe out of this world / whan god list it fall

In this stanza from the *Dialogue* 281-7 the forceful first and fourth lines and the vigorous metaphor of the *rogh besom* lose something of their power to the contrasting weakness of the other lines.

Such lines are exceptional in their attempt and their effect. Most of Hoccleve's verse remains within his modest technical control of the line, and it was probably his real awareness of this limitation compared with Chaucer's sureness of foot, as much as any conventional modesty, that led him to confess his *meetrynge amis*. None the less, his metrical competence is an accomplishment. His verse, for the most part, reads well and easily within the limited range of its emotional and imaginative scope. Here too, as in the choice of stanza and length of composition, Hoccleve's critical judgement is recognizably that of a serious, albeit minor, poet who has thought about his art.

The influence of Chaucer

In all aspects of Hoccleve's poetry the influence of Chaucer is readily apparent. Before his death in 1400, from which time nothing of Hoccleve's verse certainly survives, this influence was personal and encouraging, as Hoccleve states. Posthumously, it worked from that personal recollection through a close reading of the *Troilus*, the *Legend of Good Women*, and the *Canterbury Tales*, towards a direct imitation of words and phrases and metres; and, more indirectly, through an expansion of some basic concepts towards the evolution of a poetic structure. The indirect influence is, of course, less certainly traceable than the direct imitation, and it may be that in some things Hoccleve owes a greater general debt to the poetic climate (albeit largely Chaucer's creation) than to specific

Chaucerian example. None the less, it is beyond doubt that Chaucer exerted the greatest influence on Hoccleve's verse. Without his example Hoccleve's achievement would have been immeasurably different in tone, quality, and shape. The four verse-forms used by Hoccleve (rhyme royal, *balade, rondeau, virelai*) are all used by Chaucer. The inspiration of at least one poem, the first *balade* addressed to Sir Henry Somer (see below, p.111) seems to spring directly from Chaucer, and Hoccleve's *virelais* most likely have a similar origin. Of these four forms the least used by Chaucer (only in his minor verse and the *Monk's Tale*, certainly early work) is the *balade*, and it may be that in his use of this stanza for the more substantial of his minor poems Hoccleve is following other models. His choice of rhyme royal, however, introduced by Chaucer and used by Hoccleve consistently in his major work, indicates the importance of Chaucer's example to his verse-forms.

Chaucer's influence has been shown above to be equally pervasive in Hoccleve's metrical patterns. Their poetry differs markedly in direction; Chaucer, unlike Hoccleve, intended his work for dramatic recitation. Yet this difference of purpose has not affected Hoccleve's metrical dependence upon Chaucer. His lines are haunted by rhythmic echoes of Chaucer's lines, as detailed examination reveals, and are directly patterned after Chaucer's use of the balanced five-stress line. This imitation includes the borrowing of words, phrases, and lines and the formation of Chaucer-like neologisms; e.g. *steerelees, brydillees, combreworldes, delauee, encombrous, equypolent, enuolupid in cryme, soules norice, Venus femel lusty children deere.* But Hoccleve's ready perception of Chaucer's linguistic skill as the *firste fyndere of our faire langage* did not lead him to attempt that concentration of meaning that produces in Chaucer both the high and the satiric style. In his religious poems and in his addresses to royal patrons, e.g. the *Modir of God* and the *balade* to the duke of York, Hoccleve's exercises in aureate diction are restrained, and elsewhere his linguistic ingenuity is limited to a dozen puns, an ear of corn beside Chaucer's bushel.

More directly copied from Chaucer, in this case the *General Prologue* 725–42, is Hoccleve's defence of broad speech in the *Dialogue* 764–7:

> Who so þat shal reherce a mannes sawe,
> As þat he seith, moot he seyn and nat varie.

For and he do, he dooth ageyn the lawe
Of trouthe, he may the wordes nat contrarie.

Similar direct echoes of Chaucer's work abound in Hoccleve's verse, giving substance to his three specific acknowledgements of *My mayster Chaucer flour of eloquence* (in the *Regiment* 1958-74, 2077-107, 4978-98) and his citations of the Wife of Bath (in the *Dialogue* 694) and the *Legend of Good Women* (in the *Letter of Cupid* 316). For example, his many complaints of penury are, at least in part, a literary convention exemplified by Chaucer's *Complaint to his purs*; the idea of writing a penance for the alleged defamation of women in the *Letter of Cupid* is discussed in the *Dialogue* 750-63 in terms which recall the Prologue to the *Legend of Good Women*, itself a conventional palinode in the tradition of Ovid's *Remedia amoris*, followed by Machaut, Nicholas de Bozon, and Jean le Fèvre; the invention of the Friend with his wayward son who in the *Dialogue* 8-28 urges Hoccleve to translate the story of Jonathas an an *exemplum* against *riot* and *foleye* most probably derives from the similarly circumstanced Franklin and the Pardoner's homily on the sins of the tavern; and the Old Man in the *Regiment*, especially lines 809-12, owes something to the Old Man in the *Pardoner's Tale*. All these imitations and borrowings give Hoccleve's verse a recognizably Chaucerian ambience and underscore the three major debts which he owes to Chaucer: the development of narrative by dialogue, the dramatic cohesion of the 'sequence', and the creation of a poetic *persona*.

The greater part of Hoccleve's verse is in direct speech, either as part of the narrative (as in the *Complaint of the Virgin*, the Prologue to the *Regiment*, the *Complaint* and the *Dialogue*, and the *Tales of Jereslaus and Jonathas*) or as a direct address by the poet to his friends and patrons. Such speech, which gives an immediacy to both narrative and exhortation, was an essential ingredient of medieval poetry, and, in England especially, narrative without dialogue is almost unknown. Chaucer's example, in one sense therefore, merely served to strengthen a predominating impulse for Hoccleve; but in another and more cogent sense, Chaucer's use of speech in all poetic contexts from the *Troilus* to the Prologue to the *Wife of Bath's Tale* gave Hoccleve definite patterns of rhythm and syntax and models of narrative technique. Thus, the exchanges between Hoccleve and Friend in the *Dialogue* 701-7 copy the controlling rapidity, the cut and thrust, of dramatic speech which is previously found only in the *Troilus*:

> 'Freend, thogh I do so, what lust or pleisir
> Shal my lord haue in þat? Noon, thynkith me.'
> 'Yis, Thomas, yis. His lust and his desir
> Is, as it wel sit to his hy degree,
> For his desport and mirthe in honestee
> With ladyes to haue daliance,
> And this book wole he shewen hem, par chance.'

Similarly, in the *Tale of Jereslaus* the empress reproves the lecherous steward in terms of idiomatic firmness which recall Pertelote or the Wife of Bath:

> 'And now to thy folie and nycetee
> Retourne woldest thow! Nay, doutelees
> It shal nat be. Stynte and holde thy pees.'

None the less, in his control of dialogue, as in all else, Hoccleve misses the subtlety of Chaucer's touch. For him, dialogue carries the narrative but rarely expresses the emotions and half-shades of meaning latent in his characters. While Hoccleve clearly learned much about the dramatic use of speech from his close reading of Chaucer, the deeper meanings eluded him.

The sequence of five poems addressed to Duke Humphrey which provides these illustrations of Hoccleve's indebtedness to Chaucer's use of dialogue also exhibits in its dramatic links the idea of the narrative cohesion of a compilation which he borrowed from the *Canterbury Tales* and perhaps, to a lesser degree, from the *Legend of Good Women*. That Hoccleve had the *Canterbury Tales* in mind when he began the 'sequence' is indicated by its opening sentence which, with a difference of season and mood, consciously echoes the famous opening of the greater poem:

> After þat hervest inned had hise sheues,
> And that the broun sesoun of Mihelmesse
> Was come, and gan the trees robbe of her leues
> That grene had ben and in lusty freisshenesse,
> And hem into colour of ȝelownesse
> Had died and doun throwen vndir foote,
> That chaunge sanke into myn herte roote.

And in the larger pattern the Friend links each of the five component poems together in a way that is reminiscent of Harry Bailey. Of course, the use of the dramatic interplay of Hoccleve and Friend as a thematic structure leading to a

wider composition exactly parallels the earler discussion be-
tween Hoccleve and the Old Man that introduced the *Regi-
ment*, but there are differences. Where the discussion in the
Regiment is confined to the Prologue, in the 'sequence' it
provides a continuous linking of all parts; in its progress it
develops a minor coherent dramatic interest as the curiosity
and comments of the Friend push Hoccleve into further
composition; and the 'sequence', like the *Canterbury Tales*,
is a *compilatio* in the technical medieval sense, a group of
loosely connected stories or extracts from diverse sources.
The working-out of this Chaucerian inspiration of the struc-
ture of the 'sequence' is one of the reasons why these poems
retain a collective vitality.

Hoccleve's greatest debt to Chaucer concerns the creation
of his poetic *persona* which is the basis of much of his verse.
In treating himself as a poetic subject Chaucer had many pre-
decessors, like Bodel, Rutebeuf, Deschamps, Muset, Chartier;
Hoccleve (as far as can be surmised) followed Chaucer only,
albeit at a distance and without that complexity of meanings
which Chaucer gave to his several *personae*. Hoccleve's por-
trayal of himself is much more unified as well as more simple.
In 1405 in *La Male Regle* he appears as an intentionally comic
figure, a sexual innocent and a gentle coward, absurdly van-
quished in life's challenges. The outer layers of this figure are
literary and Chaucerian exaggeration in the manner of
'Chaucer' in the *Canterbury Tales*; but the substrata are real
enough, and in the end the *persona* is only realizable in an
unChaucerian manner in terms of its reality, not its veri-
similitude.

In 1411 in the *Regiment* the comic overtones of the *persona*
are dropped and Hoccleve speaks seriously of his own concerns
on his own behalf, although in this expression also a number of
conventional motifs are discernible. In developing the *persona*
from its Chaucerian base towards a more literal interpretation,
which incidentally became the first occurrence of an unam-
biguous personal voice in English poetry. Hoccleve is partly
conditioned by his immediate poetic intentions. Where
Chaucer composed for his own dramatic recitation before the
court of Richard II, Hoccleve intended (and indeed had no
other choice) a private reading by his patron. While such a
reading would always have been aloud, perhaps even by one
person in a small company, it necessitated the use of a minor
key and an immediate, unsubtle clarity of address. The
comparatively large number of extant manuscripts of the

Regiment suggests that the new approach was successful. Gower too, from a different standpoint and with a much greater intellectual content and without Chaucerian inspiration, had achieved a similar impact in the *Confessio Amantis*, and it may well be that Hoccleve's *persona* in the *Regiment* owes something to that larger poem, which he had certainly read; the Old Man and the Confessor, and Hoccleve and the Lover, having some points in common alongside their wider disparities.

The final appearance of Hoccleve's *persona* in 1421 and 1422 in the *Complaint* and the *Dialogue* repeats the pattern set down in the *Regiment.* The anxiety over money has given way to a greater concern about his rejection by his acquaintance after his illness, and the Old Man is replaced in the *Dialogue* by the Friend, but a similar personal intensity leads to a similar resolve to write a book for a patron, this time a compilation set more firmly in a Chaucerian mould. Hoccleve is, no doubt, writing as it were to a formula, but the apparent artificiality of the design, even in its use of the literary convention of the Wild Man, makes the real emotions of the *persona* the more striking. In these poems, as in *La Male Regle* and the *Regiment*, he is concerned (in Eliot's phrase) to metamorphose his private failures and disappointments, and the *persona* he adopts is coherently and unambiguously his own:

> I write as my symple conceyt may peyse.
> And trustith wel, al that my penne seith
> Proceedith of good herte and trewe, in feith.
> (*Regiment* 4401-3)

The original Chaucerian inspiration, however transmuted by his own poetic and intellectual experience, is the basis of this *persona.*

In all these ways the impress of Chaucer lies clearly on Hoccleve's verse. Yet when the account is fully set down, his poetic spirit is not essentially Chaucerian at all. The flash of irony, the sparkle of doubt, the loving economy of the *mot juste*, above all the sense of the complexity of things, find no echo in his verse. His affinities are more with the intensely personal and narrower outlook of the new men, of Dunbar and Skelton. His religious passion and his cry for advancement resemble theirs, though characteristically he never runs to their excesses; and like them he uses the opportunities of his verse to resolve personal problems. Like them too, he stands directly in the main tradition of English poetry, firmly linked through translation to the European heritage yet happiest when expressing an individual variation of the main theme. While almost every line that he wrote has been influenced by Chaucer, Hoccleve stands apart from his *worthy mayster honorable*, a successor and not an imitator.

The Regiment of Princes

Hoccleve completed his major work in 1411 at the age of 43. Its theme was wholly traditional, an examination and justification of the virtues necessary to a ruler, which ultimately derived from the advice supposedly given by Aristotle to Alexander. The troubled reign of Richard II (1377-99) had given the subject an urgent topicality, and, in compiling such a treatise for Prince Henry, Hoccleve could be sure of his interest in the work both as an expression of idealism and as a manual of practical usage. Interestingly, the policy of an Anglo-French alliance reinforced by royal marriage which Hoccleve advocated in the final and largest section of the work, *De pace* (especially lines 5391-404), was adopted by Henry after the victory at Agincourt.

The *Regiment*, however, is more a tract for the times than a formal treatise on royal virtues. Though Hoccleve states his intention to 'translate' three major works (Aegidius de Columna, *De regimine principum*, the pseudo-Aristotelian *Secreta Secretorum*, and Jacob de Cessolis, *De ludo scaccorum*) in lines 2051-3 and 2109-14, these are works of reference rather than source material in the conventional sense. An analysis of the sixth section, *De misericordia* (146 lines in 21 stanzas), will illustrate his eclectic method. Mercy is defined by reference to St. Augustine and St. Matthew (both quoted in Latin in the margin) as the essential Christian virtue. It is illustrated (unhistorically, be it said) by the practice of John of Gaunt and Henry IV, the prince's grandfather and father, and it is praised by St. Bernard, St. Matthew, and Seneca (all quoted in the margin). This is followed by an *exemplum* of Pyrrus and his drunken detractors (taken from *De ludo scaccorum* ii. 23), and a final exhortation is supported by a reference to the Proverbs of Solomon (quoted in the margin) and an *exemplum* of Pisistaris' mercy towards the impetuous lover of his daughter (taken from *De ludo scaccorum* iii. 15). There is an endearing *naïveté* and lightness about all this which is remote from the normal prolixity of medieval moralizing and which makes the *Regiment* seem almost a *jeu d'esprit* beside its weightier sources. The proper 'authorities' are included, although their words are confined to the margin; two small *exempla* tell of classical occasions of royal mercy; some judicious flattery of the house of Lancaster is added for good measure; and Hoccleve has said what he wants to say *de misericordia*.

The *Regiment* has fifteen such sections of varying length: royal dignity (28 lines in 4 stanzas), the coronation oath (273 in 39), justice (308 in 44), observation of the laws (224 in 32), piety (315 in 45), mercy (147 in 21), patience (168 in 24), chastity (273 in 39), magnanimity (105 in 15), untrustworthiness of riches (119 in 17), generosity but not prodigality (350 in 50), avarice (273 in 39), prudence (112 in 16), good counsel (161 in 23), peace (420 in 60). The intellectual progression through these conditions of kingship is largely directed by Hoccleve's sources, especially Aegidius, whose work (mainly, Book I, parts 1 and 2) gives to the *Regiment* its thematic skeleton which is then fleshed out by borrowings from the other sources, but the emphasis which Hoccleve gives to some virtues in preference to others is personal. Clearly, and perhaps inevitably in the circumstances of the book's writing, he rated royal generosity among the highest of kingly attributes. This disparity of treatment prevents any writing to formula, and Hoccleve ranges without restriction as freely among topical references and homely truths as among classical *exempla*. These form, perhaps, one-third of his material, generally not extending for more than a few lines or stanzas each; the largest concerns John of Canace (25 stanzas) in the eleventh section, *De virtute largitatis*. A similar variation in the lengths of illustrative stories is found in the *Confessio Amantis*, where the seventh book concerns the education of princes, and though Hoccleve is attempting something different, Gower's example no doubt had an indirect influence.

As a handbook to the princely virtues, the *Regiment* is thus unusual. Compact, topical, so organized that its sections are easily found and read, written in Hoccleve's directly literate style, its air of light seriousness invites the reader. By contrast, Trevisa's literal prose translation of Aegidius in two hundred double-columned folios, which was available at this time, is repellently heavy. However, the seriousness of the *Regiment* is never in doubt, and by comparison with Gower (who treats of only five royal virtues: truth, liberality, justice, pity, chastity) Hoccleve deals with his subject comprehensively, even though he lacks much interest in exemplary narrative. He is indeed concerned with the political character of the next reign, where the suppression of heresy, the removal of corruption, the punishment of evil-doers, and the prompt payment of annuities are matters of equal moment. He hopes for a return to the good old days of *benyngne Edward þe laste* (line 2556), and if this is essentially an expression of conservatism it is, none the less, an articulate call for responsible government. In 1411 the young Prince of Wales must have read it, as Hoccleve intended, with great personal reference.

The seriousness of Hoccleve's personal interest in his public theme is emphasized in the lengthy Prologue (2,016 lines, two-fifths of the total) where he discusses his private anxieties with an Old Man. There is much here of literary convention (the stormy night, the despairing poet, the chance encounter with an old man whose ancient misdeeds led ultimately to pious contentment, the discussion of marriage, the advice of wisdom to youth, and the decision to write a book), and the Old Man is undoubtedly related by close cousinage to Gower's Confessor. Yet the predominant theme is expressed by Hoccleve's own authentic voice, which is skilfully harmonized with the enshrouding fiction. The Old Man, whose former dissolute life is in one sense a fearful nightmarish extension of Hoccleve's own misrule in *La Male Regle*, exemplifies in retrospect all the horrors of intemperance, after which the royal virtues set out in the main part of the book shine the more attractively: in similar juxtaposition Aegidius discusses temperance and intemperance. And the account of this former dissipation and his opinions thereon (lines 187–749), which include a sharp attack on foppish dress, enables the Old Man to act as confessor to Hoccleve, who accepts this role by his constant address of *fader*, and so advise him on his courses. Since the most obvious road to success is for Hoccleve to write down his grievances and the prince to read them, the fiction of the Prologue also achieves its private function as a plea for personal favour.

Much of the attraction of the Prologue today lies in its incidental details relating to Hoccleve's life and times, but this should not obscure the real contribution which it makes to the *Regiment* as a whole. It is, once more, craftsman's work. A similar caution and a similar praise can be extended to the complete work. It is a serious, lively, and personal expression of a thoughtful man's views on the times, and though its immediate impulses and responses are gone beyond recall, it retains its freshness and directness.

Hoccleve and Lydgate

For some twelve years, from the completion of the *Regiment* in 1411 to the completion of the 'sequence' in 1422, Hoccleve was writing as it were alongside the contemporary Lydgate (*c*.1370–1449). There is no evidence that they knew each other's work, but it is highly unlikely that Hoccleve at least, closely in touch with London bookshops and book production, was unaware of Lydgate's verse; for example, the *Siege of Thebes*, ostensibly a continuation of the *Canterbury Tales*, would certainly have attracted his attention. Their major poetic activities during these years move in parallel, and may even have been shaped by a conscious rivalry.[19] In 1411 Hoccleve presented the *Regiment* to Prince Henry; in 1412 Lydgate began the *Troy Book* (completed in 1420) for the prince. About 1414 Lydgate wrote the *Defence of Holy Church* against the Lollards; in 1415 Hoccleve wrote the *Remonstrance against Oldcastle*. In 1421 Lydgate wrote the *Epithalamium for the duke of Gloucester* and at about the same time completed the *Siege of Thebes*, possibly for Gloucester also;[20] in 1422 Hoccleve presented the 'sequence' to the duke. Coincidentally or not, these poems offer illuminating areas of comparison.

Lydgate's output is enormous, more than ten times that of Hoccleve (e.g. the *Troy Book* contains 30,000 lines, the *Siege of Thebes* 4,700 lines), and he has received correspondingly more critical attention. His literary range is wide, comprehending historical narrative and hagiography and (if the *Temple of Glas* is certainly his) dream poetry, but its expression is always prolix and artificial. His self-complacent literary conservatism breaks no new ground, and as the fif-

[19] There are a number of apparent verbal, intellectual, and metaphorical echoes of Hoccleve in Lydgate's verse which further study may confirm as direct borrowings. There is nothing in Hoccleve of Lydgate's verse. For another comparison of the two poets see E.P. Hammond, *English Verse between Chaucer and Surrey* pp.54–6.

[20] It is generally claimed that Lydgate wrote this work (which lacks date and dedication in the extant copies) for his own pleasure, but this view is untenable. No fifteenth-century English poet wrote at such length without a patron in mind; the work is a pendant to the *Troy Book*, completed for Henry V, and Gloucester as *custos Anglie* (30 December 1419–1 February 1421) was the most important man in the realm during the king's absence; its hero Tydeus is compared to Gloucester in the *Epithalamium* 138–40.

teenth century develops its own character, pushing forward to new directions, he walks out of step down a narrowing cul-de-sac. Always a churchman in good point and content with his world, conventionally religious, uncritically sententious, and essentially unmoved, he has nothing to say; he is, in his own words, *voyde of al chaunge and of nufanglenesse.* Hoccleve, on the other hand, lived more hardly and more closely to the common experiences of discontent and despair. Always eager for new things, much of his verse is concerned with contemporary translation (e.g. the *Letter of Cupid* and *Lerne to Dye*), and he was able to push the rhetorical conventions of his day towards a personal voice both for himself and (in hindsight) for English poetry. And in the end, in the final stanzas of the *Complaint*, he achieved a finer religious poetry than anything Lydgate wrote.

Both poets share a debt to Chaucer as metrical craftsmen. Lydgate is the more obviously directed to the rhetorical colouring of aureate diction and figures of speech, but lacks Hoccleve's self-criticism and sharp awareness of his capabilities. Consequently, despite hundreds of verbal echoes and imitations of Chaucer, his verse is confined by a limping artificiality and a yawning verbosity, while Hoccleve can strike out of his unaffectedness a telling metaphor and line (e.g. *rogh besom, storm of descendyng, Excesse at bord hath leyd his knyf with me, Never yit stood wiis man on my feet*) and give his verse at its most rhetorical the easy fluency of natural speech, as in this couplet from the *Remonstrance 25-6,*

> O Oldcastel! Allas, what eilid thee
> To slippe into the snare of heresie?

where apostrophe and rhetorical question, assonance and alliteration, metaphor and metre combine to give a perfect expression of meaning.

A similar difference distinguishes Lydgate and Hoccleve as narrative poets. Hoccleve is able to tell a lively story with selection and dispatch, allowing the narrative to be carried forward naturally by dialogue. Lydgate, moving crepuscularly on a massive scale, entangles his story in a thicket of irrelevant detail and unnecessary explanation and so fails to hold a clear narrative line. Hoccleve's imagination is direct and dramatic and creative, Lydgate's is static and happiest before *tableaux.* Hoccleve reads well in selection, Lydgate is too diffuse. Hoccleve speaks with a recognizably modern accent, Lydgate's voice is lifelessly medieval and in need of an interpreter.

In making these comparisons it is pertinent to ignore Lydgate's output after his election as prior of Hatfield Broad Oak in 1423, when Hoccleve had written his last line and both were about 53 years of age (that is, to treat him mainly as the author of the *Troy Book* and the *Siege of Thebes*, each intended as a Chaucerian imitation in romance epic, and to ignore the later two-thirds of his verse which includes all his hagiographies and the *Fall of Princes*), for the vastness of his production prejudices any critical assessment. Even with such an allowance, suppressing all that he wrote as an elderly man, Lydgate emerges as the less vital poet. In a word, he lacks Hoccleve's critical economy and his dominant sense of the personal interest which, whether true or feigned, is the basis of all good writing. Though both are indisputably minor poets in Chaucer's long shadow, Lydgate's greyness throws Hoccleve's brightness into a sharper relief.

Critical Reputation

In his lifetime Hoccleve enjoyed a modest reputation. He numbered among his patrons some of the highest in the land (Henry V as prince and king, Edward, duke of York, John, duke of Bedford, Humphrey, duke of Gloucester, and John of Gaunt's daughter, Joan, countess of Hereford) as well as dignitaries of the City of London. And he supported this success, like Chaucer and Gower, by overseeing the publication of his work; even in his last years he wrote out fair copies of his minor poems and the 'sequence'. Shortly after his death in 1426 a 'collected works' was formed by the addition of the *Regiment* to the 'sequence', and this large volume (extant in five manuscripts) enjoyed a vogue in the second quarter of the century, though modest in comparison with the *Regiment* (separately extant in forty other copies, mostly made after 1450).

Despite the posthumous reputation of the *Regiment*, which was on the extant evidence one of the six most popular English poems of the fifteenth century and was read and annotated in Tudor times, Hoccleve is never cited alongside Gower, Chaucer, and Lydgate. No doubt the matter of the book *De regimine principum* ensured that in politically troubled reigns it would be read, but the *Regiment* is merely one of half-a-dozen English treatises on the same theme and none of these others, in prose or verse, achieved anything like its popularity and circulation. While this may be due in part to the early establishment of the *Regiment* among courtly and government circles, much is clearly due to the easiness and readability of Hoccleve's presentation and his concern with practicalities and topicalities, rather than abstractions and classical analogues. In these formative years which led to the Tudor usurpation, the book contributed something to the national consciousness of the duties of kingship.

In the sixteenth, seventeenth, and eighteenth centuries Hoccleve became largely the concern of antiquarians like John Stow and William Browne. Apart from the *Modir of God* and the *Letter of Cupid* which were falsely ascribed to Chaucer, his work remained unprinted. Browne published an abridged and modernized version of the *Tale of Jonathas*, with an enthusiastic verse preface, in 1614, and Mason published six of the minor poems in 1796, but otherwise he was known only in manuscript and from the unflattering comments of literary historians. Thomas Wright's edition of the *Regiment* in 1860 and Furnivall's edition of the complete works in 1892-7 made him accessible once more.

In the first half of the twentieth century he is largely praised for his chattiness, damned for his false metre on indefensible grounds, and generally and patronizingly denied any competence in his craft. The outstanding exception to this dismal record of uninformed criticism was Miss Hammond, whose selection of Hoccleve's verse in 1927 was edited with sympathy and scholarship and still provides, with Furnivall's edition, the basis for modern understanding. Since 1950 Hoccleve's reputation as a poet has profited from the current reassessments of fifteenth-century literature. While he still suffers at the hands of literary historians from inherited misconceptions and inattentive reading, detailed individual studies, like those of Miss Thornley on *La Male Regle*, Mr Fleming on the *Letter of Cupid*, and Mr Robinson on his prosody, are making possible a more exact recognition of his value. Further work of this kind, especially a detailed examination of his sources and analogues, will undoubtedly enhance this understanding.

Hoccleve is, of course, a minor poet whose closeness to Chaucer vividly illuminates the narrowness of his achievement, and he offers no sudden revelations to aesthetic taste. But he is a skilled and thoughtful craftsman, and against the background of early fifteenth-century London he writes well and directly to his matter. His poetry reveals a sober, good-natured view of things, a love of order and justice, an underlying sense of piety, and a gentle and inoffensive sense of humour. It is impossible to read it and not to like it.

REFERENCE WORKS

Editions

F.J. Furnivall, *Hoccleve's Works*, EETS e.s. lxi (1892, revised by A.I.
Doyle and J. Mitchell 1970) and lxxii (1897).
I. Gollancz, *Hoccleve's Minor Poems II*, EETS e.s. lxxiii (1892, revised
1970).
E.P. Hammond, *English Verse between Chaucer and Surrey* (1927).
G. Mason, *Poems by Thomas Hoccleve* (1796).
B. O'Donaghue, *Thomas Hoccleve. Selected Poems* (1981).
T. Wright, *De Regimine Principum*, Roxburghe Club (1860).

Bibliographies

J.A.W. Bennett, 'Thomas Hoccleve' in *The New Cambridge Bibliography
of English Literature* i (1974) 646-7.
E.P. Hammond, op. cit., pp.57-60.
W. Matthews, 'Thomas Hoccleve' in A.E. Hartung, *A Manual of the
Writings in Middle English 1050-1500* iii (1972) 903-8.
J. Mitchell, *Thomas Hoccleve. A Study in Early Fifteenth-Century
English Poetic* (1968), pp.125-45, and 'Hoccleve Studies,
1965-80' in *Fifteenth-century literature. Recent essays*, ed. R.F.
Yeager (Archon Books, forthcoming).

A NOTE ON THE TEXTS

All of Hoccleve's poems survive in holograph (Huntington Library MSS HM 111 and 744, and University of Durham MS Cosin V. iii. 9) except the *Complaint* and the *Regiment of Princes.* The editing of these holograph poems necessarily follows thèse manuscripts, and the collated readings of other copies where they exist have been recorded only in those very few instances where Hoccleve's text seems to include mechanical copying errors.

The *Complaint* is edited from the text of Bodleian Library MS Selden supra 53, a carefully made posthumous copy *c.*1430, after collation with four other manuscripts, and those collations are recorded in the apparatus. The extracts from the *Regiment of Princes* are taken from British Library MS Arundel 38, one of two copies made in or shortly after 1411 under Hoccleve's supervision; the other contemporary copy, MS Harley 4866, was printed by Furnivall in 1897. As a full collation of all manuscripts will appear in the forthcoming critical edition of the *Regiment of Princes,* the textual apparatus here records only collated readings from selected manuscripts (as detailed on p.114 below) where the text of MS Arundel 38 has been amended. In the text altered letters are italicized, and added letters are enclosed within square brackets.

Scribal abbreviations in all manuscripts have been expanded in transcription. Only two call for comment, the curled final *-r* which has been expanded to *-re* and, in MS Arundel 38 only, some occurrences of the supralinear abbreviation sign for *-ur.* While vocalic *-r* is possible, the presence of forms with curled final *-r* in eye-rhyme (e.g. *suffr'* 4912) suggest that scribes intended *-re.* The scribe of MS Arundel 38 regularly uses the abbreviation sign for *-ur* in conventional environments; occasionally, in the forms *ȝouur* at lines 2004, 2037, 2074, 4288, 4290, 4905, 4913, 4965, 4968, 4973) alongside regular *ȝour,* the suprascript may indicate scribal indecision or merely *-r,* as the form *commaundou-ur* 4969 in eye-rhyme suggests. In these ambiguous forms the suprascript has been expanded as *-r,* but *ȝouur* as a graphic variant of *ȝowr* is, of course, possible.

With some hesitation, modern punctuation has been adopted as more suitable than scribal punctuation to the present intentions, which are to introduce Hoccleve to a wider audience than he now enjoys. But scribal punctuation, which is recorded in the editions of Furnivall and Hammond, has guided editorial punctuation at every line. A facsimile edition of Hoccleve's three holograph manuscripts which will show his punctuation is planned. Facsimiles of individual pages are given by Furnival, vol. 1 (1892), op. p.xxviii; Doyle and Parkes, *loc. cit.* (p.xii above), plates 53 and 54; P.J. Croft, *Autograph Poetry in the English Language* . . . (1973) i. 3–4; A.G. Petti, *English Literary Hands* . . . (1977) p.54; H.C. Schulz, 'Thomas Hoccleve, Scribe', *Speculum* xii (1937) 71–81, plates I and II.

Manuscripts of Hoccleve's poems are described in *Transactions of the Edinburgh Bibliographical Society* iv (1974) 255–97. Holograph MSS 111 and 744, written 1422–6, perhaps formed one manuscript; leaves containing other verse are now lacking. Holograph MS Cosin V.iii.9 was written for the Countess of Westmoreland 1422–6. MS Arundel 38 was written in or shortly after 1411, probably for Thomas FitzAlan, Earl of Arundel. MS Selden Supra 53, the earliest surviving 'collected works', was written *c.* 1430, perhaps for Duke Humphrey or one of his circle.

THE COMPLAINT OF THE VIRGIN

O fadir God, how fers and how cruel,
In whom thee list or wilt, canst thow thee make.
Whom wilt thow spare, ne wot I neuere a deel,
Syn thow thy sone hast to the deeth betake,
That thee offendid neuere ne dide wrake
Or mystook Him to thee or disobeyde,
Ne to noon othere dide He harm or seide.

I hadde ioye entiere and also gladnesse
Whan thow betook Him me to clothe and wrappe
In mannes flessh. I wend, in sothfastnesse,   10
Have had for euere ioye by the lappe.
But now hath sorwe caught me with his trappe.
My ioye hath made a permutacioun
With wepyng and eek lamentacioun.

O holy goost, þat art all confortoure
Of woful hertes that wofulle be
And art hire verray helpe and counceyloure,
That eek of hy vertu shadwist me
Whan þat the clernesse of thi diuinitee
So shynyng in my feerful goost alight,   20
Which þat me sore agastid and affright,

Why hast thow me not in thy remembraunce
Now at this tyme right as thow had tho?
O why is it noght vnto thi pleasaunce
Now for to shadwe me as wel also,
That hid from me myght be my sones wo?
Wherof if þat I may no confort haue,
From deethes strook there may no thing me saue.

O Gaubriel, whan þat thow came apace
And madest vnto me thy salewyng   30
And seidest thus, "Heil Mary, ful of grace",
Why ne had thow youen me warnyng
Of þat grace that veyn is and faylyng,
As thow now seest, and sey it wel beforne,
Syn my ioye is me rafte, my grace is lorne.

O thow Elizabeth, my cosyn dere,
The wordes þat thow spak in the mountayne
Be endid al in another manere
Than thow had wende. My blissyng into peyne
Retorned is. Of ioye am I bareyne.   40
I song to sone, for I sang be the morwe
And now at euene I wepe and make sorwe.

O womman þat among the peple speek,
How þat the wombe blessid was þat beer,
And the tetes þat yaf to sowken eek
The sone of God, which on hy hangith heer,
What seist thow now, why comest thow no neer?
Why n'art thow heere? O womman, where art thow
That nat ne seest my woful wombe now?

O Simeon, thow seidest me ful sooth,   50
The strook that perce shal my sones herte
My soule thirle it shal. And so it dooth.
The wownde of deeth ne may I nat asterte.
Ther may no martirdom me make smerte
So sore as this martire smertith me.
So sholde he seyn þat myn hurt mighte see.

O Ioachim, O deere fadir myn,
And seint Anne, my modir deere also,
To what entente or to what ende or fyn
Broghten yee me foorth þat am greeued so?   60
Mirthe is to me become a verray fo.
Your fadir Dauid þat an harpour was
Conforted folk þat stood in heuy cas.

My thynkith yee nat doon to me aright
Þat were his successours, syn instrument
Han yee noon left wherwith me make light
And me conforte in my woful torment.
Me to doon ese han yee no talent,
And knowen myn conforteless distresse.
Yee oghten weepe for myn heuynesse.   70

O blessid sone, on thee wole I out throwe
My salte teeres, for oonly on thee
My look is set. O thynke, how many a throwe
Thow in myn armes lay and on my knee

Thow sat and haddist many a kus of me.
Eek, thee to sowke, on my brestes yaf Y
Thee norisshyng faire and tendrely.

Now thee fro me withdrawith bittir deeth
And makith a wrongful disseuerance.
Thynke nat, sone, in me þat any breeth   80
Endure may þat feele al this greuance.
My martirdom me hath at the outrance.
I needes sterue moot syn I thee see
Shamely nakid, strecchid on a tree.

And this me sleeth, þat in the open day
Thyn hertes wownde shewith him so wyde
Þat alle folk see and beholde it may,
So largeliche opned is thy syde.
O wo is me, syn I nat may it hyde.
And among othir of my smerte greeues   90
Thow put art also, sone, amonges theeues,

As thow were an euel and wikkid wight.
And lest þat somme folk perauenture
No knowleche hadde of thy persone aright,
Thy name Pilat hath put in scripture
Þat knowe mighte it euery creature,
For thy penance sholde nat been hid.
O wo is me, þat al this see betid.

How may myn yen þat beholde al this
Restreyne hem for to shewe by weepynge   100
My hertes greef? Moot I nat weepe? O yis.
Sone, if thow haddist a fadir lyuynge
That wolde weepe and make waymentynge
For þat he hadde paart of thy persone,
That were a greet abreggynge of my mone.

But thow in eerthe fadir haddist neuere.
No wight for thee swich cause hath for to weepe
As þat haue I. Shalt thow fro me disseuere
Þat aart al hoolly myn? My sorwes deepe
Han al myn hertes ioie leid to sleepe.   110

76 Eek] Eeek   107 weepe] pleyne

No wight with me in thee, my sone, hath part.
Hoolly of my blood, deere chyld, thow art.

That doublith al my torment and my greef.
Vnto myn herte it is confusion
Thyn harm to see, þat art to me so leef.
Mighte nat, sone, the redempcioun
Of man han bee withoute effusioun
Of thy blood? Yis, if it had been thy lust.
But what thow wilt be doon, souffre me must.

O deeth, so thow kythist thy bittirnesse   120
First on my sone and aftirward on me.
Bittir art thow and ful of crabbidnesse
That my sone hast slayn thurgh thy crueltee
And nat me sleest. Certein nat wole I flee.
Come of, come of, and slee me heere as blyue.
Departe from him wole I nat alyue.

O moone, o sterres, and thow firmament,
How many yee fro wepynge yow restreyne
. And seen your creatour in swich torment?
Yee oghten troublid been in euery veyne   130
And his despitous deeth with me compleyne.
Weepeth and crieth as lowde as yee may,
Our creatour with wrong is slayn this day.

O sonne, with thy cleere bemes brighte
Þat seest my child nakid this nones tyde,
Why souffrest thow him in the open sighte
Of the folk heere vnkeuered abyde?
Thou art as moche, or more, holde him to hyde
Than Sem þat helid his fadir Noe
Whan he espyde þat nakid was he.   140

If thow his sone be, do lyk therto.
Come of, withdrawe thy bemes brightnesse.
Thow art to blame but if thow so do.
For shame hyde my sones nakidnesse.
Is ther in thee no sparcle of kyndenesse?
Remembre he is thy lord and creatour.
Now keuere him for thy worsship and honour.

O eerthe, what lust hast thow to susteene
The crois on which he þat thee made and it
Is hangid, and aourned thee with greene   150
Which þat thow werist? How hast thow thee qwit
Vnto thy lord? O do this for him yit.
Qwake for doel and cleue thow in two,
And al þat blood restore me vnto

Which thow hast dronke. It myn is and not thyn.
Or elles thus, withouten taryynge,
Tho bodyes dede whiche in thee þat lyn
Caste out, for they by taast of swich dewynge
Hem oghte clothe ageyn in hir clothynge.
Thow Caluarie, thow are namely   160
Holden for to do so. To thee speke Y.

O deere sone, myn deeth neighith faste
Syn to anothir thow hast youen me
Than vnto thee. And how may my lyf laste
Þat me yeuest any othir than thee?
Thogh he whom thow me yeuest maiden be
And thogh by iust balance thow weye al,
The weighte of him and thee nat is egal.

He a disciple is and thow art a lord.
Thow al away art gretter than he is.   170
Betwixt your mightes is ther greet discord.
My woful torment doublid is by this.
I needes mourne moot and fare amis.
It seemeth þat thow makist departynge
Twixt thee and me for ay withoute endynge,

And namely syn thow me 'woman' callist,
As I to thee straunge were and vnknowe.
Therthurgh, my sone, thow my ioie appallist.
Wel feele I þat deeth his vengeable bowe
Hath bent and me purposith doun to throwe.   180
Of sorwe talke may I nat ynow,
Syn fro my name 'I' doon away is now.

Wel may men clepe and calle me Mara
From hennesforward, so may men me call.
How sholde I lenger clept be Maria,
Syn 'I', which is Ihesus, is fro me fall.

This day al my swetnesse is into gall
Torned, syn þat 'I', which was the beautee
Of my name, this day bynome is me.

O Iohn, my deere freend, thow hast receyued   190
A woful modir, and an heuy sone
Haue I of thee. Deeth hath myn othir weyued.
How may we two the deeth eschue or shone?
We drery wightes two, wher may we wone?
Thou art of confort destitut, I see,
And so am I. Ful careful been wee.

Vnto oure hertes deeth hath sent his wownde.
Noon of vs may alleggen othres peyne.
So manye sorwes in vs two habownde
We han no might fro sorwe vs restreyne.   200
I see non othir, die moot we tweyne.
Now let vs steruen heer par compaignie.
Sterue thow there, and heere wole I die.

O angels, thogh yee mourne and waile and weepe,
Yee do no wrong. Slayn is your creatour
By the folk þat yee weren wont to keepe
And gye and lede. They to dethes shour
Han put him, thogh yee han wo and langour,
No wondir is it. Who may blame yow?
And yit ful cheer he had hem þat him slow.   210

O special loue þat ioyned haast
Vnto my sone, strong is thy knyttynge.
This day therin fynde I a bittir taast
For now the taast I feele and the streynynge
Of deeth. By thy deeth feele I deeth me stynge.
O poore modir, what shalt thow now seye?
Poore Marie, thy wit is [al] aweye.

Marie? Nay, but 'marred' I thee calle.
So may I wel, for thow art wel, I woot,
Vessel of care and wo and sorwes alle.   220
Now thow art frosty cold, now fyry hoot,
And right as þat a ship or barge or boot
Among the wawes dryueth steerelees,
So doost thow, woful womman, confortlees.

And of modir haast thow eek lost the style.
No more maist thow clept be by thy name.
O sones of Adam, al to long whyle
Yee tarien hens. Hieth hidir for shame,
See how my sone for your gilt and blame
Hangith heer al bybled vpon the crois.   230
Bymeneth him in herte and cheere and vois.

His blody stremes see now and beholde.
If yee to him han any affeccioun
Now for his wo your hertes oghten colde.
Shewith your loue and your dileccioun.
For your gilt makith he correccioun
And amendes right by his owne deeth.
That yee nat reewe on him, myn herte it sleeth.

A modir þat so soone hir cote taar
Or rente, sy men neuere noon or this,   240
For chyld which þat shee of hir body baar
To yeue her tete, as my chyld þat heere is;
His cote hath torn for your gilt, nat for his,
And hath his blood despent in greet foysoun,
And al it was for your redempcioun.   Cest tout.

Ceste conpleynte paramont feust
translatee au commandement de
ma dame de Hereford, que dieu
pardoynt

THE MOTHER OF GOD

Modir of God and virgyne vndeffouled,
O blisful queene, of queenes emperice,
Preye for me that am in synne mowled,
To God thy sone, punysshere of vice,
Þat of his mercy, thogh þat I be nyce
And negligent in keepyng of his lawe,
His hy mercy my soule vnto him drawe.

Modir of mercy, wey of indulgence,
Þat of al vertu art superlatyf,
Sauere of vs by thy beneuolence,   10
Humble lady, mayde, modir, and wyf,
Causere of pees, feyntere of wo and stryf,
My preyere vnto thy sone presente,
Syn for my gilt I fully me repente.

Benigne confort of vs wrecches alle,
Be at myn endyng whan þat I shal deye.
O welle of pitee, vnto thee I calle.
Ful of swetnesse, helpe me to weye
Ageyn the feend þat with his handes tweye
And his might plukke wole at the balance   20
To weye vs doun. Keepe vs from his nusance.

And for thow art ensaumple of chastitee
And of virgynes worsship and honour —
Among alle wommen blessid thow be —
Now speke and preye to our sauueour
Þat he me sende swich grace and fauour,
Þat al the hete of brennyng leccherie
He qwenche in me, blessid maiden Marie.

O blessid lady, the cleer light of day,
Temple of our lord and roote of al goodnesse,   30
Þat by prayere wypest cleene away
The filthes of our synful wikkidnesse,
Thyn hand foorth putte and helpe my distresse,
And fro temptacioun deliure me
Of wikkid thoght thurgh thy benignitee.

So þat the wil fulfild be of thy sone,
And þat of the holy goost he m'enlumyne,
Preye for vs, as ay hath been thyne wone.
Lady, alle swiche emprises been thyne.
Swich an aduocatrice, who can dyuyne   40
As thow — right noon — our greeues to redresse?
In thy refuyt is al our sikirnesse.

Thow shapen art by Goddes ordenance
Mene for vs, flour of humilitee.
Ficche þat, lady, in thy remembrance
Lest our fo, the feend, thurgh his sotiltee,
þat in awayt lyth for to cacche me,
Me ouercome with his treecherie.
Vnto my soules helthe thow me gye.

Thow art the way of our redempcioun,   50
For Cryst of thee hath deyned for to take
Flessh and eek blood for this entencioun,
Vpon a crois to die for our sake.
His precious deeth made the feendes qwake
And cristen folk for to reioisen euere.
From his mercy helpe vs we nat disseuere.

Tendrely remembre on the wo and peyne
þat thow souffridist in his passioun
Whan watir and blood out of thyn yen tweyne
For sorwe of him ran by thi cheekes doun.   60
And syn thow knowest þat the enchesoun
Of his deeth was for to saue al mankynde,
Modir of mercy, þat haue in thy mynde.

Wel oghten we thee worsshipe and honure,
Paleys of Cryst, flour of virginitee,
Syn vpon thee was leid the charge and cure
The lord to bere of heuene and eerthe and see
And alle thynges þat therynne be.
Of heuenes kyng thow art predestinat
To hele our soules of hir seek estat.   70

Thy maidens wombe in which our lord lay,
Thy tetes whiche him yaf to sowke also

60 thi] this

To our sauynge, be they blessid ay.
The birthe of Cryst our thraldom putte vs fro.
Ioie and honour be now and eueremo
To him and thee þat vnto libertee
Fro thraldam han vs qwit. Blessid be yee.

By thee, lady, ymakid is the pees
Betwixt angels and men, it is no doute.
Blessid be God þat swich a modir chees.   80
Thy gracious bountee spredith al aboute.
Thogh þat oure hertes steerne been and stoute,
Thow to thy sone canst be swich a mene
That alle our giltes he foryeueth clene.

Paradys yates opned been by thee,
And broken been the yates eek of helle.
By thee the world restored is, pardee.
Of al vertu thow art the spryng and welle.
By thee al bountee, shortly for to telle,
In heuene and eerthe by thyn ordenance   90
Parforned is, our soules sustenance.

Now syn thow art of swich auctoritee,
Lady pitous, virgyne wemmelees,
þat our lord God nat list to werne thee
Of thy requeste, I wot wel doutelees.
Than spare nat foorth thee to putte in prees
To preye for vs, Crystes modir deere.
Benygnely wole he thyn axyng heere.

Apostle and freend familier of Cryst
And his ychosen virgyne, seint Ion,   100
Shynynge apostle and euangelyst,
And best beloued among hem echon,
With our lady preye I thee to been oon
þat vnto Cryst shal for vs alle preye.
Do thus for vs, Crystes derlyng, I seye.

Marie and Ion, heuenely gemmes tweyne,
O lightes two shynyng in the presence
Of our lord God, now do your bysy peyne
To wasshe away our cloudeful offense,
So þat we mowen make resistence   110

Ageyn the feend and make him to bewaille
Þat your preyere may so moche auaille.

Yee been the two, I knowe verraily,
In which the fadir God gan edifie,
By his sone oonly geten specially,
To him an hows. Wherfore I to yow crye,
Beeth leches of our synful maladie.
Preyeth to God, lord of misericorde,
Oure olde giltes þat he nat recorde.

Be yee oure help and our proteccioun   120
Syn, for meryt of your virginitee,
The priuilege of his dileccioun
In yow confermed God vpon a tree
Hangyng, and vnto oon of yow seide he
Right in this wyse, as I reherce can,
"Beholde heere, lo thy sone, womman."

And to þat othir, "Heer thy modir, lo."
Than preye I thee þat for the greet swetnesse
Of the hy loue þat God twixt yow two
With his mowth made and of his noblesse   130
Conioyned hath yow thurgh his blisfulnesse,
As modir and sone, helpe vs in our neede
And for our giltes make oure hertes bleede.

Vnto yow tweyne I my soule commende,
Marie and Iohn, for my sauuacioun.
Helpith me þat I may my lyf amende.
Helpith now þat the habitacioun
Of the holy goost, our recreacioun,
Be in myn herte now and eueremore,
And of my soule wasshe away the sore.   Amen.   140

LA MALE REGLE DE T. HOCCLEUE

O precious tresor inconparable!
O ground and roote of prosperitee!
O excellent richesse, commendable
Abouen alle þat in eerthe be!
Who may susteene thyn aduersitee,   5
What wight may him auante of worldly welthe,
But if he fully stande in grace of thee,
Eerthely god, piler of lyf, thow Helthe?

Whil thy power and excellent vigour
As was plesant vnto thy worthynesse   10
Regned in me and was my gouernour,
Than was I wel, tho felte I no duresse,
Tho farsid was I with hertes gladnesse.
And now my body empty is and bare
Of ioie and ful of seekly heuynesse,   15
Al poore of ese and ryche of euel fare.

If þat thy fauour twynne from a wight,
Smal is his ese and greet is his greuance.
Thy loue is lyf, thyn hate sleeth doun right.
Who may conpleyne thy disseuerance   20
Bettre than I þat of myn ignorance
Vnto seeknesse am knyt, thy mortel fo?
Now can I knowe feeste fro penaunce,
And whil I was with thee kowde I nat so.

My grief and bisy smert cotidian   25
So me labouren and tormenten sore
Þat what thow art now, wel remembre I can,
And what fruyt is in keepynge of thy lore.
Had I thy power knowen or this yore,
As now thy fo conpellith me to knowe,   30
Nat sholde his lym han cleued to my gore
For al his aart, ne han me broght thus lowe.

But I hauc herd men seye longe ago,
Prosperitee is blynd and see ne may,
And verifie I can wel it is so   35

For I myself put haue it in assay.
Whan I was weel, kowde I considere it? Nay.
But what, me longed aftir nouelrie
As yeeres yonge yernen day by day,
And now my smert accusith my folie.   40

Myn vnwar yowthe kneew nat what it wroghte,
This woot I wel, whan fro thee twynned shee.
But of hir ignorance hirself shee soghte
And kneew nat þat shee dwellyng was with thee;
For to a wight were it greet nycetee   45
His lord or freend wityngly for t'offende,
Lest þat the weighte of his aduersitee
The fool oppresse and make of him an ende.

From hennes foorth wole I do reuerence
Vnto thy name and holde of thee in cheef,   50
And werre make and sharp resistence
Ageyn thy fo and myn, þat cruel theef
þat vndirfoote me halt in mescheef,
So thow me to thy grace reconcyle.
O now thyn help, thy socour, and releef,   55
And I for ay misreule wole exyle.

But thy mercy excede myn offense,
The keene assautes of thyn aduersarie
Me wole oppresse with hir violence.
No wondir thogh thow be to me contrarie,   60
My lustes blynde han causid thee to varie
Fro me thurgh my folie and inprudence;
Wherfore I, wrecche, curse may and warie
The seed and fruyt of chyldly sapience.

As for the more paart youthe is rebel   65
Vnto reson and hatith hir doctryne:
Regnynge which, it may nat stande wel
With yowthe, as fer as wit can ymagyne.
O yowthe, allas! Why wilt thow nat enclyne
And vnto reuled resoun bowe thee,   70
Syn resoun is the verray streighte lyne
þat ledith folk vnto felicitee?

Ful seelde is seen þat yowthe takith heede
Of perils þat been likly for to falle.
For haue he take a purpos þat moot neede   75

Been execut, no conseil wole he calle;
His owne wit he deemeth best of alle,
And foorth therwith he renneth brydillees,
As he þat nat betwixt hony and galle
Can iuge, ne the werre fro the pees.   80

Alle othir mennes wittes he despisith;
They answeren no thyng to his entente.
His rakil wit only to him souffysith.
His hy presumpcioun nat list consente
To doon as þat Salomon wroot and mente,   85
Þat redde men by conseil for to werke.
Now youthe, now thow sore shalt repente
Thy lightlees wittes dulle, of reson derke.

My freendes seiden vnto me ful ofte
My misreule me cause wolde a fit,   90
And redden me in esy wyse and softe
A lyte and lyte to withdrawen it.
But þat nat mighte synke into my wit,
So was the lust yrootid in myn herte,
And now I am so rype vnto my pit   95
Þat scarsely I may it nat asterte.

Who so cleer yen hath and can nat see,
Ful smal of ye auaillith the office.
Right so, syn reson youen is to me
For to discerne a vertu from a vice,   100
If I nat can with resoun me cheuice
But wilfully fro reson me withdrawe,
Thogh I of hire haue no benefice,
No wondir, ne no fauour in hir lawe.

Reson me bad and redde as for the beste   105
To ete and drynke in tyme attemprely,
But wilful youthe nat obeie leste
Vnto þat reed, ne sette nat therby.
I take haue of hem bothe outrageously
And out of tyme nat two yeer or three   110
But twenty wyntir past continuelly.
Excesse at borde hath leyd his knyf with me.

The custume of my repleet abstinence,
My greedy mowth, receite of swich outrage,

And hondes two, as woot my negligence,   115
Thus han me gyded and broght in seruage
Of hire þat werreieth euery age;
Seeknesse, Y meene, riotoures whippe,
Habundantly þat paieth me my wage,
So þat me neithir daunce list ne skippe.   120

The outward signe of Bachus and his lure
Þat at his dore hangith day by day
Excitith folk to taaste of his moisture
So often þat man can nat wel seyn nay.
For me, I seye I was enclyned ay   125
Withouten daunger thidir for to hye me,
But if swich charge vpon my bak lay
That I moot it forbere as for a tyme.

Or but I were nakidly bystad
By force of the penylees maladie;   130
For thanne in herte kowde I nat be glad
Ne lust had noon to Bachus hows to hie.
Fy! lak of coyn departith conpaignie,
And heuy purs with herte liberal
Qwenchith the thristy hete of hertes drie,   135
Wher chynchy herte hath therof but smal.

I dar nat telle how þat the fressh repeir
Of Venus femel lusty children deere,
Þat so goodly, so shaply were and feir,
And so plesant of port and of maneere,   140
And feede cowden al a world with cheere,
And of atyr passyngly wel byseye,
At Poules Heed me maden ofte appeere
To talke of mirthe and to disporte and pleye.

Ther was sweet wyn ynow thurghout the hous   145
And wafres thikke, for this conpaignie
Þat I spak of been sumwhat likerous.
Where as they mowe a draght of wyn espie,
Sweete and in wirkynge hoot for the maistrie
To warme a stomak with, therof they drank.   150
To suffre hem paie had been no courtesie;
That charge I took to wynne loue and thank.

Of loues aart yit touchid I no deel;
I cowde nat, and eek it was no neede.
Had I a kus I was content ful weel,   155
Bettre than I wolde han be with the deede.
Theron can I but smal, it is no dreede.
When þat men speke of it in my presence
For shame I wexe as reed as is the gleede.
Now wole I torne ageyn to my sentence.   160

Of him þat hauntith tauerne of custume
At shorte wordes the profyt is this:
In double wyse his bagge it shal consume
And make his tonge speke of folk amis,
For in the cuppe seelden fownden is   165
Þat any wight his neigheburgh commendith.
Beholde and see what auantage is his
Þat God, his freend, and eek himself offendith.

But oon auantage in this cas I haue.
I was so ferd with any man to fighte,   170
Cloos kepte I me, no man durste I depraue,
But rownyngly I spak nothyng on highte.
And yit my wil was good, if þat I mighte
For lettynge of my manly cowardyse,
Þat ay of strokes impressid the wighte,   175
So þat I durste medlen in no wyse.

Wher was a gretter maister eek than Y,
Or bet aqweyntid at Westmynstre Yate?
Among the tauerneres namely
And cookes whan I cam eerly or late,   180
I pynchid nat at hem in myn acate
But paied hem as þat they axe wolde;
Wherfore I was the welcomere algate
And for a verray gentil man yholde.

And if it happid on the someres day   185
Þat I thus at the tauerne hadde be,
Whan I departe sholde and go my way
Hoom to the Priuee Seel, so wowed me
Hete and vnlust and superfluitee
To walke vnto the brigge and take a boot   190
Þat nat durste I contrarie hem alle three
But dide as þat they stired me, God woot.

And in the wyntir, for the way was deep,
Vnto the brigge I dressid me also
And ther the bootmen took vpon me keep,   195
For they my riot kneewen fern ago.
With hem I was itugged to and fro,
So wel was him þat I with wolde fare;
For riot paieth largely eueremo,
He styntith neuere til his purs be bare.   200

Othir than maistir callid was I neuere
Among this meynee in myn audience.
Me thoghte I was ymaad a man foreuere.
So tikelid me þat nyce reuerence
Þat it me made largere of despense   205
Than þat I thoghte han been. O flaterie,
The guyse of thy traiterous diligence
Is folk to mescheef haasten and to hie.

Al be it þat my yeeres be but yonge,
Yit haue I seen in folk of hy degree   210
How þat the venym of faueles tonge
Hath mortified hir prosperitee,
And broght hem in so sharp aduersitee
Þat it hir lyf hath also throwe adoun.
And yit ther can no man in this contree   215
Vnnethe eschue this confusioun.

Many a seruant vnto his lord seith
Þat al the world spekith of him honour,
Whan the contrarie of þat is sooth, in feith,
And lightly leeued is this losengeour,   220
His hony wordes, wrappid in errour,
Blyndly conceyued been, the more harm is.
O thow fauele, of lesynges auctour,
Causist al day thy lord to fare amis.

Tho combreworldes clept been enchantours   225
In bookes as þat I haue or this red,
That is to seye sotil deceyuours,
By whom the peple is misgyed and led
And with plesance so fostred and fed
Þat they forgete hemself and can nat feele   230

227 deceyuours] deceyuous

The soothe of the condicion in hem bred
No more than hir wit were in hire heele.

Who so þat list in the Book of Nature
Of Beestes rede, therin he may see,
If he take heede vnto the scripture   235
Where it spekth of meermaides in the see,
How þat so inly mirie syngith shee
Þat the shipman therwith fallith asleepe
And by hire aftir deuoured is he.
From al swich song is good men hem to keepe.   240

Right so the feyned wordes of plesance
Annoyen aftir, thogh they plese a tyme
To hem þat been vnwyse of gouernance.
Lordes, beeth waar, let nat fauel yow lyme;
If þat yee been enuolupid in cryme,   245
Yee may nat deeme men speke of yow weel.
Thogh fauel peynte hir tale in prose or ryme,
Ful holsum is it truste hir nat a deel.

Holcote seith vpon the book also
Of Sapience, as it can testifie,   250
Whan þat Vlixes saillid to and fro
By meermaides, this was his policie:
Alle eres of men of his conpaignie
With wex he stoppe leet, for þat they noght
Hir song sholde heere, lest the armonye   255
Hem mighte vnto swich deedly sleep han broght;

And bond himself vnto the shippes mast.
Lo, thus hem alle saued his prudence.
The wys man is of peril sore agast.
O flaterie! O lurkyng pestilence!   260
If sum man dide his cure and diligence
To stoppe his eres fro thy poesie,
And nat wolde herkne a word of thy sentence,
Vnto his greef it were a remedie.

A nay! Althogh thy tonge were ago   265
Yit canst thow glose in contenance and cheere.
Thow supportist with lookes eueremo
Thy lordes wordes in eche mateere,
Althogh þat they a myte be to deere.

And thus thy gyse is priuee and appert 270
With word and look among our lordes heere
Preferred be, thogh ther be no dissert.

But whan the sobre, treewe, and weel auysid
With sad visage his lord enfourmeth pleyn
How þat his gouernance is despysid 275
Among the peple, and seith him as they seyn,
As man treewe oghte vnto his souereyn
Conseillynge him amende his gouernance,
The lordes herte swellith for desdeyn
And bit him voide blyue with meschance. 280

Men setten nat by trouthe nowadayes,
Men loue it nat, men wole it nat cherice,
And yit is trouthe best at alle assayes.
Whan þat fals fauel, soustenour of vice,
Nat wite shal how hir to cheuyce, 285
Ful boldely shal trouthe hir heed vp bere.
Lordes, lest fauel yow fro wele tryce,
No lenger souffre hire nestlen in your ere.

Be as be may, no more of this as now,
But to my misreule wole I refeere. 290
Wher as I was at ese weel ynow,
Or excesse vnto me leef was and deere
And or I kneew his ernestful maneere,
My purs of coyn had resonable wone,
But now therin can ther but scant appeere. 295
Excesse hath ny exyled hem echone.

The feend and excesse been conuertible,
As enditith to me my fantasie.
This is my skile, if it be admittible:
Excesse of mete and drynke is glotonye; 300
Glotonye awakith malencolie;
Malencolie engendrith werre and stryf;
Stryf causith mortel hurt thurgh hir folie.
Thus may excesse reue a soule hir lyf.

No force of al this, go we now to wacche 305
By nyghtirtale out of al mesure.
For as in þat fynde kowde I no macche
In al the Priuee Seel with me to endure,

And to the cuppe ay took I heede and cure
For þat the drynke apalle sholde noght.   310
But whan the pot emptid was of moisture,
To wake aftirward cam nat in my thoght.

But whan the cuppe had thus my neede sped
And sumdel more than necessitee,
With repleet spirit wente I to my bed   315
And bathid ther in superfluitee.
But on the morn was wight of no degree
So looth as I to twynne fro my cowche
By aght I woot. Abyde, let me see.
Of two as looth I am seur kowde I towche.   320

I dar nat seyn Prentys and Arondel
Me countrefete and in swich wach go ny me,
But often they hir bed louen so wel
Þat of the day it drawith ny the pryme
Or they ryse vp. Nat telle I can the tyme   325
Whan they to bedde goon, it is so late.
O helthe lord, thow seest hem in þat cryme,
And yìt thee looth is with hem to debate.

And why I not? It sit nat vnto me,
Þat mirrour am of riot and excesse,   330
To knowen of a goddes pryuetee,
But thus I ymagyne and thus I gesse:
Thow meeued art of tendre gentillesse
Hem to forbere, and wilt hem nat chastyse
For they in mirthe and vertuous gladnesse   335
Lordes reconforten in sundry wyse.

But to my purpos. Syn þat my seeknesse
As wel of purs as body hath refreyned
Me fro tauerne and othir wantonnesse,
Among an heep my name is now desteyned.   340
My greuous hurt ful litil is conpleyned,
But they the lak conpleyne of my despense.
Allas, þat euere knyt I was and cheyned
To excesse, or him dide obedience.

Despensee large enhaunce a mannes loos   345
Whil they endure; and whan they be forbore
His name is deed, men keepe hir mowthes cloos

As nat a peny had he spent tofore.
My thank is qweynt, my purs his stuf hath lore,
And my carkeis repleet with heuynesse.   350
Be waar, Hoccleue, I rede thee therfore,
And to a mene reule thow thee dresse.

Who so passynge mesure desyrith,
As þat witnessen olde clerkes wyse,
Himself encombrith often sythe and myrith.   355
And forthy let the mene thee souffyse.
If swich a conceit in thyn herte ryse,
As thy profyt may hyndre or thy renoun
If it were execut in any wyse,
With manly resoun thriste thow it doun.   360

Thy rentes annuel, as thow wel woost,
To scarse been greet costes to susteene,
And in thy cofre pardee is cold roost.
And of thy manuel labour, as I weene,
Thy lucre is swich þat it vnnethe is seene   365
Ne felt. Of yiftes seye I eek the same.
And stele, for the guerdoun is so keene,
Ne darst thow nat ne begge also for shame.

Than wolde it seeme þat thow borwid haast
Mochil of þat þat thow haast thus despent   370
In outrage and excesse and verray waast.
Auyse thee, for what thyng þat is lent
Of verray right moot hoom ageyn be sent;
Thow therin haast no perpetuetee.
Thy dettes paie, lest þat thow be shent   375
And or þat thow therto conpellid be.

Sum folk in this cas dreeden more offense
Of man for wyly wrenches of the lawe
Than he dooth eithir God or conscience,
For by hem two he settith nat an hawe.   380
If thy conceit be swich, thow it withdrawe,
I rede, and voide it clene out of thyn herte
And first of God and syn of man haue awe,
Lest þat they bothe make thee to smerte.

380 an] om.

Now lat this smert warnynge to thee be,   385
And if thow maist heer aftir be releeued,
Of body and purs so thow gye thee
By wit þat thow no more thus be greeued.
What riot is, thow taastid haast and preeued.
The fyr, men seyn, he dreedith þat is brent,   390
And if thow so do, thow art wel ymeeued.
Be now no lenger fool, by myn assent.

Ey, what is me þat to myself thus longe
Clappid haue I? I trowe þat I raue.
A, nay. My poore purs and peynes stronge   395
Han artid me speke as I spoken haue.
Who so him shapith mercy for to craue,
His lesson moot recorde in sundry wyse,
And whil my breeth may in my body waue,
To recorde it vnnethe I may souffyse.   400

O god, o Helthe, vnto thyn ordenance,
Weleful lord, meekly submitte I me.
I am contryt and of ful repentance
Þat euere I swymmed in swich nycetee
As was displesaunt to thy deitee.   405
Now kythe on me thy mercy and thy grace,
It sit a god been of his grace free.
Foryeue and neuere wole I eft trespace.

My body and purs been at ones seeke,
And for hem bothe I to thyn hy noblesse   410
As humblely as þat I can byseeke
With herte vnfeyned reewe on our distresse.
Pitee haue of myn harmful heuynesse.
Releeue the repentant in disese.
Despende on me a drope of thy largesse,   415
Right in this wyse if it thee lyke and plese.

Lo, lat my lord the Fourneval, I preye,
My noble lord þat now is tresoreer,
From thyn hynesse haue a tokne or tweye
To paie me þat due is for this yeer   420
Of my yeerly ten poundes in th'eschequeer,
Nat but for Michel terme þat was last.

421 ten pound] x. li.

I dar nat speke a word of ferne yeer,
So is my spirit symple and sore agast.

I kepte nat to be seen inportune   425
In my pursuyte; I am therto ful looth.
And yit þat gyse ryf is and commune
Among the peple now withouten ooth;
As the shamelees crauour wole, it gooth,
For estaat real can nat al day werne.   430
But poore shamefast man ofte is wroth;
Wherfore for to craue moot I lerne.

The prouerbe is, the doumb man no lond getith.
Who so nat spekith and with neede is bete
And thurgh arghnesse his owne self forgetith,   435
No wondir thogh anothir him forgete.
Neede hath no lawe, as þat the clerkes trete,
And thus to craue artith me my neede,
And right wole eek þat I me entremete,
For þat I axe is due, as God me speede.   440

And þat that due is, thy magnificence
Shameth to werne as þat I byleeue.
As I seide, reewe on myn impotence,
þat likly am to sterue yit or eeue
But if thow in this wyse me releeue.   445
By coyn I gete may swich medecyne
As may myn hurtes alle þat me greeue
Exyle cleene and voide me of pyne.

BALADE TO MASTER JOHN CARPENTER

See heer, my maistre Carpenter, I yow preye,
How many chalenges ageyn me be
And I may nat deliure hem by no weye,
So me werreyeth coynes scarsetee
That ny cousin is to necessitee.   5
Forwhy vnto yow seeke I for refut
Which þat of confort am ny destitut.

Tho men whos names I aboue expresse
Fayn wolden þat they and I euene were,
And so wolde I, God take I to witnesse.   10
I woot wel I moot heere or elleswhere
Rekne of my dettes and of hem answere.
Myn herte for the dreede of God and awe
Fayn wolde it qwyte — and for constreynt of lawe.

But by my trouthe nat wole it betyde,   15
And therfore as faire as I can and may
With aspen herte I preye hem abyde
And me respyte to sum lenger day.
Some of hem grante and some of hem seyn nay,
And I so sore ay dreede an aftirclap   20
That it me reueth many a sleep and nap.

If þat it lykid vnto your goodnesse
To be betwixt [hem] and me swich a mene
As þat I mighte kept be fro duresse,
Myn heuy thoghtes wolde it voide clene.   25
As your good plesance is this thyng demene.
How wel þat yee doon and how soone also,
I suffre may in qwenchynge of my wo.   Cest tout.

1–3 *adds in margin* A de B et C de D et cetera Ceste balade feust
tendrement considere et bonement execute   23 hem] *om.*

BALADES TO SIR HENRY SOMER

Cestes balade et chanceon ensuyantz feurent faites a mon Meistre H. Somer quant il estoit Souztresorer

The sonne with his bemes of brightnesse
To man so kyndly is and norisshynge
That lakkyng it day nere but dirknesse.
Today he yeueth his enlumynynge
And causith al fruyt for to wexe and sprynge.
Now syn þat sonne may so moche auaille
And moost with somer is his soiournynge,
That sesoun bonteuous we wole assaille.

Glad cheerid Somer, to your gouernaille
And grace we submitte al our willynge. 10
To whom yee freendly been he may nat faille
But he shal haue his resonable axynge.
Aftir your good lust, be the sesonynge
Of our fruytes this laste Mighelmesse,
The tyme of yeer was of our seed ynnynge,
The lak of which is our greet heuynesse.

We truste vpon your freendly gentillesse,
Ye wole vs helpe and been our suppoaille.
Now yeue vs cause ageyn this Cristemesse
For to be glad. O lord, whethir our taille 20
Shal soone make vs with our shippes saille
To Port Salut. If yow list we may synge,
And elles moot vs bothe mourne and waille
Til your fauour vs sende releeuynge.

We your seruantes, Hoccleue and Baillay,
Hethe and Offorde, yow byseeche and preye,
Haastith our heruest as soone as yee may.
For fere of stormes our wit is aweye.
Were our seed inned, wel we mighten pleye
And vs desporte and synge and make game. 30
And yit this rowndel shul we synge and seye
In trust of yow and honour of your name.

Somer, þat rypest mannes sustenance
With holsum hete of the sonnes warmnesse,
Al kynde of man thee holden is to blesse.

Ay thankid be thy freendly gouernance
And thy fressh look of mirthe and of gladnesse.
Somer, etc.

To heuy folk of thee the remembrance
Is salue and oynement to hir seeknesse.
For why we thus shul synge in Cristemesse,
Somer, etc.

Ceste balade ensuyante feust, par la Court de Bone Conpaignie,
enuoiee a lonure sire Henri Somer, Chaunceller de leschequer
et vn de la dite court.

Worshipful sire, and our freend special
And felawe in this cas we calle yow.
Your lettre sent vnto vs cleerly al
We haue red, and vndirstanden how
It is no wit to your conceit, as now,
Vse the rule foorth as we been inne,
But al anothir rule to begynne;

Rehercynge how in the place of honour,
The Temple, for solace and for gladnesse,
Wheras nat oghte vsid been errour   10
Of ouer mochil waast or of excesse,
First wern we fowndid to vse largesse
In our despenses; but for to exceede
Reson, we han espyed yee nat beede.

Yee allegge eek how a rule hath be kept
Or this which was good, as yee haue herd seyn,
But it now late cessid hath and slept,
Which good yow thynkith were vp take ageyn.
And but if it so be, our court certeyn
Nat likly any whyle is to endure,   20
As hath in mowthe many a creature.

Yee wolden þat in conseruacioun
Of oure honour and eek for our profyt,
Þat th'entente of oure old fundacioun
Obserued mighte been and to þat plyt
Be broght as it was first and passe al qwyt
Out of the daunger of outrageous waast,
Lest with scorn and repreef feede vs swich taast.

Vnto þat ende sixe shippes grete
To yeue vs han yee grauntid and behight,   30
To bye ageyn our dyner flour or whete,
And besyde it, as reson wole and right,
Paie your lagh as dooth anothir wight,
Þat by mesure rulith him and gyeth,
And nat as he whom outrage maistrieth.

In your lettre contened is also
Þat if vs list to chaunge in no maneere
Our newe gyse ne twynne therfro,
The firste day of May yee wole appeere —
Þat day yee sette be with vs in feere —   40
And to keepe it yee wole be reedy.
This is th'effect of your lettre soothly.

To the whiche in this wyse we answere.
Excesse for to do be yee nat bownde,
Ne noon of vs, but do as we may bere.
Vpon swich rule we nat vs ne grownde.
Yee been discreet, thogh yee in good habownde.
Dooth as yow thynkith for your honestee.
Yee and we alle arn at our libertee.

At our laste dyner wel knowen yee   50
By our stywardes limitacioun,
As custume of our court axith to be,
And ay at oure congregacion
Obserued, left al excusacion,
Warned yee wern for the dyner arraye
Ageyn Thorsday next, and nat it delaye.

We yow nat holde auysid in swich wyse
As for to make vs destitut þat day
Of our dyner. Take on yow þat empryse.
If your lust be, dryueth excesse away.   60

Of wyse men mochil folk lerne may.
Discrecion mesurith euery thyng.
Despende aftir your plesance and lykyng.

Ensaumpleth vs, let seen, and vs miroure
As þat it seemeth good to your prudence.
Reule þat day, for the thank shal be youre.
Dooth as yow list be drawe in consequence.
We trusten in your wys experience.
But keepith wel your tourn, how so befalle,
On Thorsday next, on which we awayte alle. Cest tout.

THREE ROUNDELS

Cy ensuent trois chaunceons, lune conpleynante a la dame
monnoie, et lautre la reponse dele a cellui qui se conpleynt,
et la tierce la commendacion de ma dame.

Wel may I pleyne on yow, lady moneye,
Þat in the prison of your sharp scantnesse
Souffren me bathe in wo and heuynesse
And deynen nat of socour me purueye.

    Whan þat I baar of your prison the keye
    Kepte I yow streite? Nay, God to witnesse.
    Wel may I pleyne, etc.

    I leet yow out. O, now of your noblesse
    Seeth vnto me, in your deffaute I deye.
    Wel may I pleyne, etc.   10

    Yee saillen al to fer. Retourne, I preye,
    Conforteth me ageyn this Cristemesse.
    Elles I moot in right a feynt gladnesse
    Synge of yow thus and yow accuse and seye,
    Wel may I pleyne, etc.

Hoccleue, I wole it to thee knowen be,
I, lady moneie, of the world goddesse,
Þat haue al thyng vndir my buxumnesse,
Nat sette by thy pleynte risshes three.

    Myn hy might haddest thow in no cheertee   20
    Whyle I was in thy slipir sikirnesse.
    Hoccleue, I wole it, etc.

    At instance of thyn excessif largesse
    Becam I of my body delauee.
    Hoccleue, I wole it, etc.

    And syn þat lordes grete obeien me,
    Sholde I me dreede of thy poore symplesse?
    My golden heed akith for thy lewdnesse.

Go, poore wrecche. Who settith aght by thee?
Hoccleue, I wole it, etc.

Of my lady wel me reioise I may.
Hir golden forheed is ful narw and smal.
Hir browes been lyk to dym reed coral.
And as the ieet hir yen glistren ay.

   Hir bowgy cheekes been as softe as clay
   With large iowes and substancial.
   Of my lady, etc.

   Hir nose a pentice is, þat it ne shal
   Reyne in hir mowth thogh shee vprightes lay.
   Of my lady, etc.

   Hir mowth is nothyng scant with lippes gray.
   Hir chin vnnethe may be seen at al.
   Hir comly body shape as a footbal.
   And shee syngith ful lyk a papeiay.
   Of my lady, etc.

THE REGIMENT OF PRINCES

The Sleepless Night

Musynge vpon the restlees bysynesse
Whyche that thys troubly world haþ ay on honde,
That oþer thyng than fruyt of bytirnesse
Ne 3yldeth nou3t as I can vnderstonde,
At Chestres Yn ry3t fast by the Stronde
As I lay in my bedde vpon a ny3t
Thog3t me berefte of slepe the force and my3t.

And many a day and ny3t that wykkyd hyne
Had before vexid my pore goost
So greuously that of anguysch and pyne   10
No rycher man was nowhere in no coost.
Thys dare I seyn may no wy3t make his bost
That he wyth thou3t was bet than I aqueyntyd,
For to the deth he wel ny hath me feyntyd.

Bysily in my mynde I gan revolue
The welthe vnseur of euery creature,
How ly3tly that fortune yt can dissolue
Whan that hyre lust that yt no lenger dure.
And of the brotelnesse of hyre nature
My tremblyng herte so grete gastnesse hadde   20
That my spyrites were of my lyf sadde.

Me fyl to mynde how that no3t long agoo
Fortunes stroke doun threst estat real
Into meschef, and I tok heede also
Of many another lord that hadde a fal.
In mene estat eke sykernesse at al
Ne sawe I non, but I se at[te] laste
Where seuretee for to abyde hyr caste.

In pore estat sche pighte hyr pauyloun
To keuer here fro the storm of descendyng,   30

1-56 H *lacks text*   11 rycher] D riche   14 he] D it ny] ne
15 gan] D can   27 atte] at   29 pore] D the pore

For sche knewe no lower descension
Sauf onli deth, fro whyche no wyȝt leuyng
Diffende hym may. And thus in my musyng
I destitute was of ioye and good hope,
And to myn ese nothyng coude I grope.

For ryȝt as blyue ranne yt in my thouȝt,
Thoghe pore I be, ȝyt sumwhat'lese I may.
Than demed I that seurte wolde nouȝt
Whyt me abyde, yt ys not to here pay,
There to soiourne as sche descende may.   40
And thus vnsyker of my smal lyflode,
Thouȝt leyde on me ful many an heuy lode.

I thouȝt eke yf I into pouerte crepe
Than am I entred into sykernesse.
But swyche seurete myȝt I ay waylle and wepe,
For pouerte bredyþ nouȝt but heuynesse.
Alas, wher ys thys worldes stabilnesse?
Here vp, here doun, heer honure, heer repreef,
Now hool, now seke, now bountee, now myschyf.

And whan I hadde rollyd vp and doun   50
Thys worldys stormy wawes in my mynde,
I sy wel pouert was exclusioun
Of al welfare regnynge in mankynde,
And how in bokes thus I wryten fynde,
The werste kynde of wrecchednesse ys
A man to han be weleful or thys.

Alas, thouȝte I, what sykernesse ys that
To lyue ay seur of gref and of nusaunce?
What schal I do? Best ys I stryf not
Ageyn þe peys of fortunes balaunce,   60
For wel I wot that hyre brotel constaunce
A wyȝt no whyle suffre can soiourne
In o plyt. Thus nat wyst I hou to turne.

For whanne a man weneth stonde most constant,
Thanne ys he next to hys ouerthrowyng;
So flyttyng ys sche and so variant,

37 pore I be] D I be poore   51 worldys] D world
58 nusaunce] *corrected from* myschaunce   60 peys] H pays

There is no triste vpon hyre fayre lawhyng.
After glad loke sche schapyþ hyre to stynge.
I was adrad so of hyre gerynesse
That my lyf was but a dedly gladnesse.   70

Thus ylke ny3t I walwyd to and fro
Sekyng reste, but certeynly sche
Appeeryd nou3t, for þoght, my cruel fo,
Chaced hadde hyre and sleepe away fro me.
And for I scholde not alone be
Ageyn my lust, wach profrid hys seruyse,
And I admyttyd hym in heuy wyse.

So long a ny3t ne felte I neuer non
As was that same to my iugement.
Who so that þou3ty ys, ys wo begon.   80
The thou3tful wy3t ys vessel of turment.
Ther nys no gref to hym equypolent.
He graueth deppest of seekenesse alle.
Ful wo ys hym that in swyche þou3t ys falle.

What why3t that inly pensyf is, I trowe
Hys most desyre ys to be solytarie.
That þys is soþ, in my persone I knowe,
For euere whyl that fretynge aduersarie
Myn herte made to hym trybutarie
In sowkynge of the fresschest of my blood,   90
To sorwe soule me thou3te yt dede me good.

For the nature of heuynesse ys thys.
If yt habunde gretly in a wyth,
The place eischewyt he where as ioye ys,
For ioye and he not mow acorde ary3t.
As discordant as day ys vnto ny3t,
And honure aduersarie is vnto schame,
Is heuynes so to ioye and game.

Whan to the thou3tful wy3t ys tolde a tale,
He herit yt as thou3 he þennes were.   100
Hys heuy þou3tys hym so plukke and hale
Hydyr and thyder and hym greue and dere

That hys eres avayle hym nat a pere.
He vnderstondeþ noþyng what men seye,
So ben hys wyttys fer gon hem to pleye.

The smert of thouȝt I by experience
Knowe as wel as any man doth lyuynge.
Hys frosty swoot and fyry hote feruence
And troubly dremes, drempt al in wakynge,
My mazyd hed sleplees han of konnyng   110
And wyt despoylyd, and so me be-iapyd
That after deth ful often haue I gapyd.

The Troubles of a Scrivener

He that neuere knew the swetnesse of wele,
Thogh he yt lakke ay, lesse hym greue yt schal
Than hym that hath ben weleful yeerys fele,
And in effect hath feeld no greef at al.   970
O pouert, God me schylde fro thy fal.
O deth, thy strook ȝyt ys more agreable
To me than lyue a lyf so miserable.

Sixe marc ȝeerly and no more than that,
Fader, to me me thynkyth ys ful lyte,
Consideryng how that I am nouȝt
In housbondrye ilerned worth a myte.
Scarsely kowde I charre away the kyte
That me byreue wolde my pullaylle.
And more axit housbondly gouernaylle.   980

Wyth plow can I nouȝt medlen ne with harwe,
Ne woot nouȝt what lond good ys for what corne,
And for to lade a cart or fylle a barwe,
To whyche I neuer vsyd was toforn,
My bakke vnbuxum hath swyche thyng forsworn
At instaunce of wrytyng, hys werreour,
That stowpyng hath hym spylt with hys labour.

Many men, fader, weenen that wrytyng
No trauaile ys, they hold hyt but a game.
Art hath no foo but swyche folk vnkunnyng.   990
But who so lyst dysporte hym in þat same

974 Sixe] vi.   984 was] H vas

Let hym continue and he schal fynde yt grame.
It ys wel gretter labour than yt semeth.
The blynde man of colours al wrong demeth.

A wryter moot thre thynges to hym knytte,
And in tho may be noo disseueraunce.
Mynde, ye, and hande, non may fro other flytte
But in hem moot be ioynt continuance.
The mynde al hool wythouten variaunce
On ye and hand awayte moot alway,   1000
And they two eke on hym, yt ys no nay.

Who so schal wryte may nouȝt holde a tale
Wyth hym and hym, ne synge thys ne that,
But al hys wyttys hoole grete and smale
There most appere and halden them therat.
And syn he speke may ne synge nat,
But bothe two he nedys moot forbere,
Hys labour to hym ys th'elengere.

Thys artificers se I day by day
In the hootteste of al hyre bysynesse   1010
Talken and singe and make game and play
And forth hyr labour passyth with gladnesse.
But we laboure in trauayllous stilnesse.
We stowpe and stare vpon the schepys skyn
And kepe must oure song and wordys in.

Wrytyng also doth grete anoyes three,
Of whyche ful fewe folkes taken hede,
Sauf we oureself, and thyse lo þey be.
Stomak ys on, whom stowpyng out of drede
Annoyeth sore. And to oure bakkes nede   1020
Moot yt be greuous. And the thrid, oure yen
Vpon the whyte mochel sorwe dryen.

The Old Man's Advice and Hoccleve's Address

'What schal I calle the? What ys þy name? '
'Hoccleue, fadir myn, men clepen me.'
'Hoccleue, sone? ' 'Iwys, fader, þat same.'

1001 no] noþ   1003 and] and wyth   4 al] of al
8 th'elengere] the lengere   12 forth] H for   21 be] H om.
22 sorwe] H for to

'Sone, I haue herd or thys men speke of the.
Thou were aqueyntyd with Chaucer, pardee.
God haue hys soule best of any wyght.
Sone, I wol holde the that I haue hight.

'Althogh thou seye that thow in Latyn   1870
Ne in Frensch nowder canst but smal endyte,
In Englyssch tonge canstow wel afyn.'
'Fader, therof can I eke but a lyte.'
'ȝe? Strawe, let be, thy penne take and wryte
As þou canst, and thy sorwe turne schal
Into gladnesse, I doute yt naght at al.

'Syn thow mayst noȝt be payd in [th'Ex]chequere,
Vnto my lord the Prince make instaunce
That þy patent into the Hanaper
May chaunged be.' 'Fader, by ȝoure suffrance,   1880
It may noȝt so bycause of th'ordenaunce,
Longe after thys schal no graunt chargeable
Out passe. Fader myn, thys ys no fable.

'An egal change, my sone, ys in soothe
No charge. I wot yt wel inow, in dede.
What, sone myn, good hert take vnto the.
Men seyn, who so of euery gras hath drede
Let hym be war to walke in eny mede.
Assay, assay, thow simpyl hertyd gost.
What grace ys schapen the, thou noȝt ne wost.'   1890

'Fadir, as syker as I stande here,
Whether that I be simple or argh or bolde,
Swyche an eschange gete I noon to yere,
Do as I can wyth that I haue in holde,
For as for that my comfort ys but colde.
But wel I fynde ȝour good wyl alway
Redy to me in what ȝe can and may.'

'That ys sothe, sone. Now syn thow me toldyst
My lord the Prince ys good lord the to,
No maistry yt ys for the, if þow woldyst,   1900
To be releeued. Wostow what to do?
Wryte to hym a goodly tale or two

1867 Chaucer] H Caucher   77 th'Exchequere] chequer'
87 gras] H grace

On whyche he may desporten hym by nyght,
And hys free grace schal vpon the lyght.

'Scharpe thi penne and write on lustyli.
Let se, my sone, make yt fresch and gay.
Out thyn art yf thow canst craftily.
Hys hye prudence hath insyghte verray
To iuge if yt be wel imaade or nay.
Wherefor, sone, yt ys vnto the nede   1910
Vnto thy werk tak the gretter heede.

'But of o thyng be wel war in al wyse,
On flaterye that thou the nouȝt founde.
For therof, sone, Salamon the wyse
As that I haue in his prouerbis founde,
Seith thus, they that in feyned speche habounde
And glosyngly vnto hir freendes talke,
Spreden a net byforne hem where they walke.

'If a deceyuour ȝeue a man to sowke
Wordes plesaunt in hony al bywrapped,   1920
Good ys a man eschew swich a powke.
Thurgh fauel hath ful many a man myshappyd,
For when that he hath ianglyd al and clappyd
Wyth hys freend, tretyng of pees openly,
He in awayt lith of hym couertly.

'The moost lakke that han the lordes grete
Is of hym that hir soothes schold hem telle.
Al in the glose folk laboure and swete,
They stryuen who best ryng schal the belle
Of fals plesaunce, in that hir hertes swelle   1930
If that oon can bet than other deceyue.
And swich deceyt lordes blyndly receyue.

'The worldly riche men han no knowliche
What þat þey ben of hyr condicion,
They ben so blent wyth fauelles gay speche,
Whyche reportith to hem þat hir renoun
Is euerywhere halwyd in the toun,
That in hemself they demen gret vertu,
Where as there ys but smal or nouȝt a gru,

1927 hym] H hem

'For vnneth a good word men speke of hem.   1940
Thys fals treson comen ys and ryf.
Bet were yt the ben at Ierusalem,
Sone, than thou were in yt defectyf.
Syn my lord the prynce is — God hold hys lyf —
To the good lord, good seruant thow þe quyte
To hym and trew, and yt schal the profite.

'Write hym nothyng that sowneth into vice.
Kythe thy loue in matere of sadnesse.
Loke if thow fynde canst eny tretyce
Groundid on his estates holsumnesse.   1950
Swyche thyng translate and vnto hys hynes
As humblely as þat thow canst present.
Do thus, my sone.' 'Fadir, I assent,

'Wyth hert as tremblyng as the leef of asp.
Fadir, syn ȝe me rede do so,
Of my simple conceyt wol I the clasp
Vndo, and lat yt at his large go.
But weleway, so ys myn hert wo
That the honour of Englyssch tong is deed,
Of which I wont was han consail and reed.   1960

'O mayster dere and fadir reuerent,
My mayster Chaucer, flour of eloquence,
Mirrour of fructuous entendement,
O vniuersel fader in science,
Allas, that thou thyn excellent prudence
In thy bed mortel mightyst noȝt byquethe.
What eiled deth? Allas, why wolde he sle the?

'O deth, thou dedyst nouȝt harm synguleer
In slaghtree of hym, but al þis land yt smertith.
But natheles ȝyt hastow no power   1970
Hys name sle. Hys hye vertu aster[t]yth
Vnslayn fro the, whych ay vs lyfly hertyth
Wyth bokes of hys ornat endytyng
That ys to al thys land enlumynyng.

1941 comen] H comon   44 hold] H help
55 do] H to do   63 entendement] endendement
70, 75 hastow] H hast þou   71 Hys] He   astertyth] asteryth

'Hastow nou3t eeke my mayster Gower slayn,
Whos vertu I am insufficient
For to descryue? I woot wel in certayn
For to sleen al thys world thou hast iment.
But syn oure lord Cryst was obedient
To the, in feyth I can no ferthere seye.   1980
Hys creatures mosten the obeye.

'Fadir, ye may lawghe at my lewde speche
If that 3ow lyst. I am nothyng fourmeel.
My yong konnyng may non hyer reche.
My wytte ys also slyper as an eel.
But how I speke, algate I mene wel.'
'Sone, thou seyst wel inow, as me semeth.
Non other fele I, so my conceyt deemeth.

'Now farewel, sone, go hom to thy mete.
It ys hye tyme, and go wyl I to myn.   1990
And what I haue iseyd the nou3t forgete.
And swych as that I am, sone, I am thyn.
Thou seest wel, age hath put me to decline
And pouert hath me maad of good al bare.
I may nou3t but prey for thy welfare.'

'What, fader, wolden 3e thus sodenly
Depart fro me? Peter! Crist forbede.
3e schal go dyne wyth me truly.'
'Sone, at o word I moot go fro the nede.'
'Nay, fader, nay.' '3ys, sone, as God me spede.'   2000
'Now, fader, synt yt may non othere tyde,
Almy3te God 3ow saue and be your gyde,

'And graunt grace me that day to see
That I sumwhat may quyte 3our goodnesse.
But, good fadir, whanne and wher schul 3e
And I efte meete? ' 'Sone, in soothfastnesse
I euery day heere at the Carmes messe,
It faylyth nou3t, aboute the houre of seuene.'
'Wel, fader, God betake I 3ow of heuene.'

1978 iment] H ment   82 lewde] H nice   83 3ow] H þow
85 ys] H om.   2001 synt] H syn   2 be] H he
7-51 H lacks leaf

Recordyng in my mynde the lesson   2010
That he to me yaf, I hom to mete wente.
And on the morwe set I me adoun,
And penne and ynke and parchemen I hente,
And to parforme hys wylle and hye entente
I took corage, and whyles yt was hote
Vnto my lord the Prince thus I wrote.

Hye noble and my3tty Prince excellent,
My lord the Prince, o my lord gracious,
I, humble seruant and obedient
Vnto 3our estate hye and glorious   2020
Of whyche I am ful tendre and ful gelous,
Me recommaunde vnto 3oure worthynesse
Wyth herte entere and spirit of meeknesse,

Ry3t humbly axyng of 3ow licence
That wyth my [penne I] may to 3ow declare,
So as that can my wyttes innocence,
Myn inward wylle that thrystyth the welfare
Of 3our persone; and els be I bare
Of blysse whan þat the cold strook of deth
My lyf hath queynt and me byreft my breth.   2030

Thogh that my lyflode and possession
Be scant, I ryche am of beneuolence.
To 3ow therof can I be no nygon.
Good haue I noon by whyche 3our excellence
May plesed be. And for myn impotence
Stoppyth the wey to do as I were holde,
I wryte as he þat 3our good lyf fayn wolde.

Aristotle, moost famous phylosofre,
Hys episteles to Alisaundre sente,
Whos sentence ys wel bet þan gold in cofre   2040
And more holsum groundyd on trewe entente.
For al that euere thoo episteles mente
To sette was thys worthy conquerour
In reule how to susteyne hys honour.

2014 to] D *om.*   20 hye] D *om.*   25 penne I] *om.*
26 as . . . wyttes] D þat my wittes kan   35 for] D *om.*
42 thoo] D þe

The tendre loue and the feruent cheerte
That thys worthy clerk ay to thys kyng bere,
Thrystynge hys welthe durable to be,
Vnto hys herte stak and sat so neer
That by wrytyng hys counsel yaf he cleer
Vnto hys lord to keepe him fro nusaunce, 2050
As wytnessyth hys book of gouernaunce.

Of which and of Gyles, of regiment
Of princes, plotmel thynke I to translate.
And thogh that simple by my sentement,
O worthy prince, I ȝow byseeche algate
Considereth how enditynge hath in hate
My dul conceyt and nat acorde may
Wyth my chyldhode, I am so childissch ay.

Also byseche I that the altitude
Of ȝour estat, thogh þat þys pamfilet 2060
Non ordre holde ne in hym include,
Nat greued be, for I can do no bet.
Anothir day whan wyt and I be met,
Whyche longe ys to, and han vs freendly kyst,
Discouere I wol that now ys nat wyst.

Nathales swyche as ys my smal connyng,
Wyth also trewe an herte I wol yt oute
As tho two dide or euere clerk lyfynge.
But tremblynge ys my spyrit, out of doute,
That to parforme that I am aboute. 2070
Allas, the stuf of sad intelligence
Me faillyth to speke in so hye presence.

Symple ys my goost and scars my letterure
Vnto ȝour excellence for to write
Myn inward loue. And ȝit aventure
Wil I me putte, thogh I can but lyte.
My dere mayster — God ys soul quyte —
And fadir, Chaucer, fayn wolde han me taght,
But I was dul and lerned lyte or naght.

46 thys] D his   50 him] hem   52 H *resumes*
54 that] H *om.*   55 ȝow] now
2067 Wyth also] H Withal so an] H and   73 ys] as   75 ȝit] H yit in

Alas, my worthy mayster honorable,   2080
Thys landes verray tresour and rychesse,
Deth by thy deth [hath] harme irriparable
Vnto vs don. Hir vengeable duresse
Despoyled hath this land of the swetnesse
Of rethorik, for vnto Tullius
Was nere man so lyk amonges vs.

Also, who was hier in philosophye
To Aristotle in our tonge but þou?
The steppes of Virgile in poesie
Thow filwedist eek. Men wot wel inow   2090
That combreworld þat þee, my mayster, slow.
Wolde I slayn were! Deth was to hastyf
To renne on the reue the þy [l]yf.

Deth hath but smal consideracion
Vnto the vertuous I haue espyed —
No more, as schewyth the probacion,
Than to a vycyous mayster losel tried
Among an heep. Euery man ys maystried
Wyth here, as wel the poore as ys þe ryche.
Leered and lewde eek standen al ilyche.   2100

Sche myȝtte han taried hir vengeance a while
Til that sum man had egal to þe be.
Nay, let be þat. She knewe wel þat þys ile
May neuere man forth brenge lyk to þe,
And hyre office nedes do moot sche.
God bad hire soo, I truste, as for thi beste.
O maister, maister! God þy soule reste.

John of Canace

Of fool largesse wol I talke a space.   4180
How yt befil, Y not in what contree,
But þere was oon named Iohn of Canace,
A ryche man, and two douȝtres had hee
That two worthy men of a citee
He wedded leet, and þere was gladnesse
And reuel more than I can expresse.

2082 hath] *om.*   86 nere] H neuer   93 lyf] *1st letter erased*
2100 Leered] H lerd ilyche] i leche   4184 two] H to two

The fadir hys doghtres and hir housbondes
Loued ful wel and hadde hem leef and dere.
Tyme to tyme he ȝaf hem wyth hys hondes
Of hys good passyngly, and they swyche chere 4190
Hym made and were of so plesant manere
That he ne wyste how be bettre at ese,
They cowden hym so wel cherice and plese.

For he as mochil haunted in partie
Hir hous as þat he did hys owne hous.
They heeld hym vp so wyth hyr flaterie
That of despenses he was outrageous,
And of hys good they were ay desirous.
Al that they axeden hadden þey redy.
They euere weren vppon hym gredy. 4200

Thys sely man continued his outrage
Tyl al hys good was disshed and gon.
And whan þey felte hys dispenses aswage
They wax vnkynde vnto hym anoon.
For after had he cherisschynge non,
They wery weren of his companye.
And he was wys and schoop a remedye.

He to a marchaunt gooth of his notise,
Whyche that his trusty frend had ben ful ȝore,
Besechynge hym þat he wolde hym cheuyse 4210
Of ten thousand pound, no lengere ne more
Than dayes þre, and he wolde yt restore
At his day. This was doon. Þe somme he hente
And to hys owne hous þerwyth he wente.

And on the morwe preyde he to souper
Hys sones bothe and hys douȝtres also.
They to hym cam wythouten any daungere.
How that þey ferden, lat it passe and go.
They ferden wel wythouten wordes moo.
To hys konnyng he greet desport hem made, 4220
He dyde hys myȝt to chere hem and to glade.

4197 despenses] H dispens   98 hys] H om.
204 vnkynde vnto hym] H to him vnkynde   7 And] H om.
4212 restore] restorye   15 morwe] H morne   18 it] H I

After souper whan they hyr tyme sy,
They took hir leue and home they wolde algate,
And he answerde and seyde hem sykerly,
'Thys nyȝt ȝe schul nat passe out of the ȝate.
ȝour hous is fer and yt ys derke and late.
Neuene yt nat, for yt schal noȝt betyde.'
And so al nyght he made hem for to abyde.

The fadir loged hem of sly purpos
In a chamber next vnto hys ioynynge,   4230
For bytwixt hem nas ther but a parcloos
Of borde nouȝt but of an homly makynge,
Thoruȝout the whiche at many a chynnyng
In eche chambre þey myȝtten beholde
And see what other dyden if þey wolde.

I can nouȝt seyn how þey slepten þat nyȝt,
Also yt longyþ noȝt to my matere.
But on the morwe at þe brode day lyȝt
The fadir roos, and for they schulden here
What þat he dyde, in a boistous manere   4240
Vnto his chyste whiche þre lokkys hadde
He wente, and þereat wrythed he ful sadde.

And whanne yt was i-opned and vnschyt
The bagge[d] gold by the marchaunt hym lent
He hath vncofred, and streyght forth wyth yt
Vnto hys beddes feet gon ys and went.
What dooth þan thys fel man and prudent,
But out thys gold on a tapyt hath schot
That in the bagges lefte þer no grot.

And al thys dyde he nouȝt but for a wyle,   4250
As that ȝe schul wel knowen aftirward
He schope hys sones and douȝtres bygyle.
Hys noyse made hem dressen hem vpward.
They caste hyr eres to hys chambreward
And herde of gold þe russchynge and the soun
As þat he rudely threw hem adoun.

28 for] H *om.*   24, 29 hem] hym   32 an] H *om.*
37 longyþ] H logith   38 pe] H *om.*   42 wrythed] H wrested
44 bagged] bagge   48 tapyt] H tippet   53 hem] hym

And to the parcloos they hem haste and hye
To wyte and knowe what hir fader wroghte.
In at the chynes of the bord þey prye
And sygh how he among the nobles soghte   4260
If deffectif were any as hem þoghte,
And on hys nayle he threw hym ofte and caste
And bagged hem and cofred at the laste,

And opneth hys dore and doun goth hys way.
And after blyue out of hyr bed þey rese
And cam doun eke. Hir fadir þanken þey
Of hys good cheere in hyr beste wyse,
And al was for the goldys couetyse,
And to gon hom þey axen of hym leue.
They ben departyd and þey there hym leue.   4270

Walkynge homward þey iangeled fast and speeke
Of the gold whyche þey sygh hir fadir haue.
On sayde, 'I wondre þeron.' 'And I eeke,'
Quod another, 'for also God me saue,
3ysterday þogh I scholde into my graue
Han crept, I durste on hyt han layde my lyf
That gold wyth hym nou3t hadde be so ryf.'

Now lat hem muse on that what so hym lyste,
And to hire fadere now wol I me dresse.
He al thys gold takyþ out of hys chyste   4280
And to the marchaunt paide yt more and lesse,
Thankynge hym ofte of hys kyndenesse.
And þennes goth he hom vnto hys mete,
And to hys sonnes hous whan he hadde i-ete.

Whan he cam þyder, þay made of hym more
Than that þey weren wond by many fold,
So grete dysport þey made hym nou3t ful 3ore.
'Fader.' quod they, 'þys ys 3our owne housholde.
In feyth þer ys nothyng withinne oure holde
But yt schal be at 3our comaundement.   4290
Wolde God that 3e were of oure assent.

Thanne we schulden ay togedre dwelle.'
Al what þey mente wyst he wel inow.

4264 opneth] H opned   82, 85, 87 hym] hem
86 wond] H wont   91 were] H werest

'Sones and douȝtres,' quod he, 'sooth to telle,
My wylle ys good also to be with ȝow.
How scholde I meryer be, nouȝt woot I how,
Than with ȝow for to be contynuel.
Ȝoure companye lykeþ me ful wel.'

Now schope yt so they helde hous in fere,
Sauf the fader. And as þey lowgh and pleyde   4300
Hys douȝtres bothe wyth lawhynge cheere
Vnto hyr fader spake and þus they seyde
And to soyle hyr questyon hym prayde,
'Now good fader, how mochel moneye
In ȝour strong bounden chyste is, we ȝow prey.'

'Ten thousand pounde,' he seyde and lyed lowde.
'I tolde hem,' quod he, 'nat ful longe agoo,
And that as redily as that I cowde.
If ȝe wol aftyr þys do to me so
As ȝe han don byforn, þanne alle tho   4310
I in my testament dispose schal
For ȝoure profyt. Ȝoures yt schal ben al.'

After þys day they alle in oon hous were
Tyl the day cam of the fadres dyenge.
Good mete and drynke and clothis for to were
He hadde, [and] payed nouȝt to hys endyng.
Whan he segh þe tyme of hys departyng,
Hys sones and hys douȝtres dyde he calle,
And in þys wyse he spaak vnto hem alle.

'Naȝt purpose I make oþer testament   4320
But of þat ys in my stronge chyste ibounde.
And ryȝt anon, or I be hennes hent,
An hundred pound of noblis good and rounde
Takyþ to Prechours, taryeþ it no stounde.
An hundred pound eek to the Freeres Greye,
And Carmes fifty. Tarye yt noght, I seye.

'And whan I buryed am of hem, the keyes
Of my chyste takyth, for they hem kepe.
By euery keye wryten ben the weyes
Of my wyl.' This gold was nouȝt suffred slepe.   4330

4303 soyle] H assoile   6 lyed] *in margin,* leed *in text*
16 and] *om.*   27 keyes] H key

It was anoon dalt, for hyre hertes depe
Stak in hys bounden cofre, and al hyre hope
Was good bagges þerynne for to grope.

To euery chyrche and reclus of the toun
[He] bad hem eeke of gold ȝeue a quantite.
Al as he bad þey weren prest and boun
And did hyt blyue. But, so moot I the,
Ful slely he deseyuyd thys meyne,
His sones and his douȝtris bothe I mene.
Her beerdes schaued he ryȝt smothee and clene.   4340

Whan he was deed and hys exequies do,
Solempnely they to the freris ȝyde
And bade tho keyes delyuere hem vnto,
And as that they hym beden, so they dyde.
Tho ioyeful sones dresse hem to the stide
Whereas þys strong bounden chiste stode.
But or they twynned þennes þey pekkyd mood.

They opneden the chyste and founde ryȝt nouȝt
But a passyngly gret sargeantes mace
In whyche þer gaily maad was and iwrouȝt   4350
This same scripture: 'I Iohn of Canace
Make swyche testament here yn thys place.
Who beryth charge of other men and ys
Of hem despysed, slayn be he wyth thys.'

De consilio habendo in omnibus factis

Now purpos I to trete how to a kyng
It needful ys to do by counsel ay,   4860
Wythouten whiche good ys he do no þyng.
For a kyng ys but a man soul, parfay,
And be hys wytte neuer so good, he may
Erre and mystake hym oþer whyle among,
Whereas good counsayl may exclude a wrong.

Excellent prince, in axynge of reed
Descouereþ naght ȝoure wylle in no manere.
What þat ȝe thynke do, lat yt be deede,
As for the tyme let no word apere,

4335 He] om. H om.   44 hym] H hem   4351 This] The
53 other] wother   4863 be] H he   68 thynke] thynge

But what euery man seyth wel herkene and here,   4870
And 3yt whan good counsayl ys 3euen 3ow,
What 3e do wole, kepe yt close inow,

Tyl þat 3ow lyke parforme hyt in dede.
And if hyt schal be don, let yt nou3t tarye,
For þat ys perylous, withoute drede.
Ther ys nothyng may make a lond myscarie
More þanne swyche delay; ful necessarye
Is it a good purpos parforme as blyue
And, if hyt naght be, out of mynde yt dryue.

And yf that a man of sympel degre,   4880
Or poore of byrthe or 3ong, be wel conseyle,
Admitte hys reson and take yt in gree.
Why naght, my goode lord? what schulde 3ow eyle?
But men don naght so, whereof I merueyle.
The wor[l]d fauoureth ay the ryches sawe,
Thogh that hys counsel be no3t worþ an hawe.

What he seyth vp ys to the clowdys bore.
But and the poore speke worth the tweye,
Hys seed no3t sprynge may, yt nys but lore.
They seyn 'what ys he, thys? lat hym goo pleye.'   4890
O worthy prince, beth wel waar, I preye,
That 3our hye dygnitee and sad prudence
No desdeyn haue of the poores sentence.

Thogh men contrarye eke 3oure opynyoun,
They may par cas counsele 3ow the beste.
Also 3e ben at 3our eleccioun
To do or leue yt as 3our seluen leste.
If hyt be good, impresse yt in the cheste
Of 3oure memorye and executith yt.
If yt nou3t be, to leue yt ys a wyt.   4900

And yf 3ow lyst 3oure counselere to preue,
3e feyne moot 3e han necessite
Of gold; and yf he styre 3ow and meue
3oure ieweles leye in wedde, certeyn he
Loueth 3our estat and prosperitee.

4878 Is it] H It is   79 And] H As   85 world] lord

But he that redith ȝou ȝoure peple oppresse,
He hateth ȝow certeyn, yt ys no lesse.

And if a man in tyme of swyche a nede
Of hys good ȝeue ȝow a good substaunce,
Swyche on cheryce, and els God forbede.   4910
Konneth hym þanke of hys good cheuyssaunce,
For hym ys leuere to suffre penaunce
Hymself thanne that ȝour peple scholde smerte.
There ys a preef of trewe louynge herte.

In axyng eke of reed, war of fauel.
Also war of the auariciouus,
For non of tho two can counseyl wel.
Hyr reed and counsel ys enuenemous.
They bothe ben of gold so desyrous,
They rekke noȝt what bryge here lord be ynne,   4920
So that they mow gold and syluer wynne.

And if ȝour counseyl whyche þat ȝe han take
Vnto the knoulyche or the audience
Of ȝoure fooes comen be, þan let it slake
And vtterly put yt in abstinence,
For execute yt were an imprudence.
In swyche a caas ys wysdam yt to chaunge.
Good ys ȝour counsel be to ȝour foes straunge.

Counsel may wel be lykned to a brydel
Whyche that an hors vp kepeth fro fallyng,   4930
If man do by counsel. But al an idel
Is reed yf man nouȝt folwe yt in wyrkyng.
Do noþyng reedles, do by counseylynge
Of hedes wyse, and no repentaunce
The[r] folwe ȝow schal in ȝoure gouernaunce.

Comenda[b]le ys counseyl take of the wyse
And nouȝt of fooles, for þey may noȝt loue
But swyche thyng as hem lyketh in al wyse.
Ȝoure counseler chese oure lord God aboue.
Cheesyth eeke good men, and away schoue   4940

4907 hateth] H hatheth   4925 vtterly] H witterly   26 an] H and
31 an] H in   32 yf] H om.   35 Ther] The
36 Comendable] Comendale   38 But] H And   39 chese] H chesith

The wycked whos counseyl ys deceyuable.
Thus byddyth holy wryt, yt ys no fable.

Chesyth men eke of olde experience,
Hyr wytt and intellect ys gloriouus.
Of hyr counseyl holsom ys the sentence,
The old mannes reed ys fructuouus.
War of ȝong counseyl, yt ys perylous.
Roboas fond yt so whan he forsook
Olde counseyl and vnto ȝong reed hym took.

Th'entente, woot I wel, of the ȝong man   4950
As louynge ys and trew as of the olde,
Though that he nat so wel counsayl can.
Ȝonge men stronge ben, hardy and bolde,
And more weldy to fyȝte yf they scholde.
But thogh the olde in tyme of pees or werre
Rede and counseyl, yt schal not be the werre.

He that ys fresch and lusty now thys day
By lengthe of ȝeeres schal nothyng be so.
Freschenesse and lust may nat endure alway.
Whan age ys comen he comaundeþ ho!   4960
But let se who consydereth thys, whoo?
Good ys that age sette a gouernayle
And ȝouthe yt sue. Thus may bothe avayle.

Excellent prince, eke on the holy dayes
Beth war that ȝe nouȝt ȝour counseyl holde,
As for tho dayes put hem in delayes.
Thynkeþ wel thys, ȝe wel apayd be nolde
If ȝour soget noȝt by ȝoure hestes tolde.
Ryȝt so our lord God kyng and commaundour
Of kynges alle ys wrooth with þat errour.   4970

In the longe ȝere ben worke dayes inowe,
If they be wel despent, for to entende
To counseyles. To God ȝour herte bowe
If ȝe desyre men hyr hertes bende
To ȝow. What kyng nat dredeth God offende,

4949 reed] H om.   54 yf] H if þat   55 thogh] H thow
61 whoo] H two   6&#x18; bothe] H al   66 dayes] H tymes
68 soget] H sogetes

Ne nat rekkeþ do hym desobeysaunce,
He schal be dysobeyd eke par chaunce.

The first findere of our fayre langage
Hath seyde in caas sembable and othyr moo
So hyly wel that yt ys my dotage   4980
For to expresse or touche ony of thoo.
Allas, my fader fro the world ys goo,
My worthy mayster Chaucer, hym I mene.
Be thow aduokett for hym, heuenes quene.

As þow wel knowyst, o blessyd virgine,
Wyth louyng herte and hye deuocioun
In thyn honour he wroot ful many a lyne.
O now thyn help and þyn promocioun
To God thy sone make a mocioun,
How he thy seruaunt was, mayden Marie,   4990
And lat his loue floure and fructyfie.

Al though hys lyf be queynt, þe resemblaunce
Of hym haþ in me so fresch lyflynesse
þat, to put other men in remembraunce
Of hys persone, I haue heere hys lyknesse
Don make, to þis ende in sothfastnesse
þat þei that haue of hym lest thoght and mynde
By þis peynture may aȝen hym fynde.

The ymages þat in þe chirche been
Maken folk þenke on God and on hys seyntes   5000
Whan þe ymages þei beholde and seen,
Where as vnsyghte of hem causeth restreyntes
Of thoughtes gode. Whan a thyng depeynt is
Or entailed, if men take of yt heede,
Thoght of þe lyknesse yt wol in hem breede.

Yit some holde opynyoun and sey
þat non ymages schulde imaked be.
þei erre foule and goo out of þe wey.
Of trouth haue þei scant sensibilite.
Passe ouer þat. Now blessid trinite,   5010

4985 þow] now   4990-5118 based on MS Harley 4866 fo. 88
97 lest] D loste   99 chirche] D chirches   5002 as] D oft
5 Thoght] D ogh   10 ouer] D oure

Vpon my maystres soule mercy haue.
For hym, lady, eke thy mercy I craue.

More othir þyng wolde I fayn speke and touche
Heere in þis booke. But swyche is my dulnesse,
For þat al voyde and empty ys my pouche,
Þat al my lust is queynt with heuynesse,
And heuy spirit comaundeth stilnesse.
And haue I spoke of pees, I schal be stille.
God sende vs pees, if þat yt be hys wille.

5012 eke thy mercy] D þi mercie eeke

TWO BALADES TO KING HENRY V

Ceste balade ensuyante feust mise en le fin du liure del Regiment des Princes

O litil book, who yaf thee hardynesse
Thy wordes to pronounce in the presence
Of kynges ympe and princes worthynesse,
Syn thow al nakid art of eloquence?
And why approchist thow his excellence
Vnclothid, sauf thy kirtil, bare also?
I am right seur, his humble pacience
Thee yeueth hardynesse to do so.

But o thyng woot I wel, go wher thow go.
I am so pryuee vnto thy sentence,   10
Thow haast and art and wilt been eueremo
To his hynesse of swich beneuolence.
Thogh thow nat do him due reuerence
In wordes, thy cheertee nat is the lesse.
And if lust be to his magnificence
Do by thy reed, his welthe it shal witnesse.

Byseeche him of his gracious noblesse,
Thee holde excusid of thyn innocence
Of endytynge, and with hertes humblesse,
If any thyng thee passe of negligence,   20
Byseeche him of mercy and indulgence,
And þat for thy good wil he be nat fo
To thee, þat al seist of loues feruence.
Þat knowith God, whom no thyng is hid fro. Cest tout.

Item, au roy, que dieu pardoint

Victorious kyng, our lord ful gracious,
We humble ligemen to your hynesse
Meekly byseechen yow, o kyng pitous,
Tendre pitee haue on our sharp distresse.
For but the flood of your rial largesse
Flowe vpon us, gold hath vs in swich hate

Þat of his loue and cheertee the scantnesse
Wole arte vs three to trotte vnto Newgate.

Benigne lige lord, o hauene and yate
Of our confort, let your hy worthynesse   10
Our indigences softne and abate.
In yow lyth al yee may our greef redresse.
The somme þat we in our bille expresse
Is nat excessif ne outrageous.
Our long seruice also berith witnesse,
We han for it be ful laborious.

O lige lord þat han be plenteuous
Vnto your liges of your grace algate,
Styntith nat now for to be bonteuous
To vs, your seruantz of the olde date.   20
God woot we han been ay, eerly and late,
Louynge lige men to your noblesse
Lat nat the strook of indigence vs mate,
O worthy prince, mirour of prowesse.   Cest tout.

BALADE TO EDWARD, DUKE OF YORK

Go, litil pamfilet, and streight thee dresse
Vnto the noble rootid gentillesse
Of the myghty prince of famous honour,
My gracious lord of York, to whos noblesse
Me recommande with hertes humblesse,
As he þat haue his grace and his fauour
Fownden alway, for which I am dettour
For him to preye, and so shal my symplesse
Hertily do vnto my dethes hour.

Remembre his worthynesse, I charge thee,   10
How ones at London desired he
Of me, þat am his seruant and shal ay,
To haue of my balades swich plentee
As ther weren remeynynge vnto me.
And for nat wole I to his wil seyn nay
But fulfille it as ferfoorth as I may,
Be thow an owtere of my nycetee
For my good lordes lust and game and play.

My lord byseeke eek in humble maneere
That he nat souffre thee for to appeere   20
In th'onurable sighte or the presence
Of the noble princesse and lady deere,
My gracious lady, my good lordes feere.
The mirour of wommanly excellence.
Thy cheere is naght ne haast noon eloquence
To moustre thee before hir yen cleere.
For myn honour were holsum thyn absence.

Yit ful fayn wolde I haue a messageer
To recommande me with herte enteer
To hir benigne and humble wommanhede,   30
And at the tyme haue I noon othir heer
But thee, and smal am I for thee the neer.
And if thow do it nat, than shal þat dede
Be left, and þat nat kepte I, out of drede.
My lord, nat I, shal haue of thee poweer.
Axe him licence, vpon him crie and grede.

Whan þat thow hast thus doon, than aftirward
Byseeche thow þat worthy prince Edward
Þat he thee leye apart, for what may tyde,
Lest thee beholde my maistir Picard. 40
I warne thee þat it shal be ful hard
For thee and me to halte on any syde
But he espie vs. Yit no force, abyde.
Let him looke on, his herte is to me ward
So freendly þat our shame wole he hyde.

If þat I in my wrytynge foleye
As I do ofte — I can it nat withseye —
Meetrynge amis or speke vnfittyngly,
Or nat by iust peys my sentences weye,
And nat to the ordre of endytyng obeye, 50
And my colours sette ofte sythe awry,
With al myn herte wole I buxumly
It to amende and to correcte him preye,
For vndir his correcioun stande Y.

Thow foul book, vnto my lord seye also
Þat pryde is vnto me so greet a fo
Þat the spectacle forbedith he me
And hath ydoon of tyme yore ago.
And for my sighte blyue hastith me fro
And lakkith þat þat sholde his confort be, 60
No wondir thogh thow haue no beautee.
Out vpon pryde, causere of my wo.
My sighte is hurt thurgh hir aduersitee.

Now ende I thus. The holy trinitee
And our lady, the blissid mayden free,
My lord and lady haue in gouernance
And grante hem ioie and hy prosperitee,
Nat to endur oonly two yeer or three
But a thousand. And if any plesance
Happe mighte, on my poore souffissance, 70
To his prowesse and hir benignitee,
My lyues ioie it were and sustenance. Cest tout.

BALADE TO JOHN, DUKE OF BEDFORD

Ce feust mys en le liure de Monseigneur Iohan, lors nommez, ore Regent de France et duc de Bedford.

Vnto the rial egles excellence
I, humble clerc, with al hertes humblesse,
This book presente, and of your reuerence
Byseeche I pardoun and foryeuenesse
þat of myn ignorance and lewdenesse
Nat haue I write it in so goodly wyse
As þat me oghte vnto your worthynesse.
My yen hath custumed bysynesse
So daswed þat I may no bet souffyse.

I dreede lest þat my maistir Massy,   10
þat is of fructuous intelligence,
When he beholdith how vnconnyngly
My book is metrid, how raw my sentence,
How feeble eek been my colours, his prudence
Shal sore encombrid been of my folie.
But yit truste I þat his beneuolence
Conpleyne wole myn insipience
Secreetly, and what is mis rectifie.

Thow book by licence of my lordes grace,
To thee speke I, and this I to thee seye.   20
I charge thee, go shewe thow thy face
Beforn my seid maistir and to him preye
On my behalue þat he peise and weye
What myn entente is þat I speke in thee,
For rethorik hath hid fro me the keye
Of hir tresor, nat deyneth hir nobleye
Dele with noon so ignorant as me.   Cest tout.

26 Of hir] Of his

MORE BALADES TO KING HENRY V

Ceste balade ensuante feust faite au tres noble roy Henri le
Quint (que Dieu pardoint) le iour que les seigneurs de son
roialme lui firent lour homages a Kenyngtoun

The Kyng of kynges regnyng ouer al.
Which stablisshid hath in eternitee
His hy might, þat nat varie he may ne shal,
So constant is his blisful deitee,
My lige lord, this grace yow graunte he,　　　　　5
That your estaat rial, which þat this day
Haath maad me lige to your souereyntee,
In reule vertuous continue may.

God dreede and ficche in him your trust verray;
Be cleene in herte and loue chastitee;　　　　　10
Be sobre, sad, iust, trouthe obserue alway;
Good conseil take, and aftir it do yee;
Be humble in goost, of your tonge attempree,
Pitous and merciable in special,
Prudent, debonaire, in mesure free,　　　　　15
Nat ouerlarge, ne vnto gold thral.

Be to your liges also sheeld and wal;
Keepe and deffende hem from aduersitee;
Hir wele and wo in your grace lyth al;
Gouerneth hem in lawe and equitee;　　　　　20
Conquere hir loue and haue hem in cheertee;
Be holy chirches champioun eek ay;
Susteene hir right, souffre no thyng doon be
In preiudice of hir, by no way.

Strengthe your modir in chacyng away　　　　　25
Th'errour which sones of iniquitee
Han sowe ageyn the feith, it is no nay.
Yee therto bownde been of duetee;
Your office is it now, for your seurtee,
Souffret¹ nat Crystes feith to take a fal.　　　　　30
Vnto his peple and youres cheerly see
In conseruyng of your estat real.

Syn God hath sent yow wit substancial
And kynges might, vertu putte in assay.
And lige lord, thogh my conceit be smal   35
And nat my wordes peynte fressh and gay
But clappe and iangle foorth, as dooth a iay,
Good wil to yow shal ther noon faille in me,
Byseechyng vnto God þat, to his pay,
Yee may gouerne your hy dignitee.   Amen.

Ceste balades ensuyantes feurent faites au tresnoble roy H.
le Quint (que Dieu pardoint) et au tres honurable conpaignie
du Iarter.

To yow, welle of honur and worthynesse,
Our right Cristen kyng, heir and successour
Vnto Iustinians deuout tendrenesse
In the feith of Ihesu, our redemptour,
And to yow, lordes of the garter, flour   5
Of chiualrie as men yow clepe and calle,
The lord of vertu and of grace auctour
Graunte the fruyt of your loos nat appalle.

O lige lord, þat han eek the liknesse
Of Constantyn, th'ensaumple and the mirour   10
To princes alle, in loue and buxumnesse
To holy chirche, o verray sustenour,
And piler of our feith and werreyour
Ageyn the heresies bittir galle,
Do foorth, do foorth, continue your socour   15
Holde vp Crystes baner, lat it nat falle.

This yle or this had been but hethenesse,
Nad been of your feith the force and vigour.
And yit this day the feendes fikilnesse
Weeneth fully to cacche a tyme and hour   20
To haue on vs, your liges, a sharp shour
And to his seruiture vs knytte and thralle.
But ay we truste in yow, our protectour.
On your constance we awayten alle.

Commandith þat no wight haue hardynesse,   25
Our worthy kyng and Cristen emperour,
Of the feith to despute more or lesse
Openly among peple where errour
Spryngith al day and engendrith rumour.
Makith swich lawe and for aght may befalle,   30
Obserue it wel therto been yee dettour.
Dooth so, and God in glorie shal yow stalle.

THE REMONSTRANCE AGAINST OLDCASTLE

Ceste feust faicte au temps que le Roy Henri le V^t (que Dieu
pardoint) feust a Hampton sur son primer passage vers Harflete.

The laddre of heuene, I meene charitee,
Comandith vs if our brothir be falle
Into errour to haue of him pitee,
And seeke weyes in our wittes alle
How we may him ageyn to vertu calle.   5
And in gretter errour ne knowe I noon
Than thow, þat dronke haast heresies galle
And art fro Crystes feith twynned and goon.

Allas, þat thow þat were a manly knyght
And shoon ful cleer in famous worthynesse,   10
Standynge in the fauour of euery wight,
Haast lost the style of cristenly prowesse
Among alle hem þat stande in the cleernesse
Of good byleeue — and no man with thee holdith
Sauf cursid caitifs, heires of dirknesse.   15
·For verray routhe of thee myn herte coldith.

Thow haast maad a fair permutacion
Fro Crystes lore to feendly doctryne
From honour and fro dominacion
Vnto repreef and mescheuous ruyne,   20
Fro cristen folk to hethenly couyne,
Fro seuretee vnto vnsikirnesse,
Fro ioie and ese vnto wo and pyne,
Fro light of trouthe vnto dirk falsnesse.

O Oldcastel! Allas, what eilid thee   25
To slippe into the snare of heresie?
Thurgh which thow foo art to the Trinitee
And to the blissid virgyne Marie
And to the innumerable holy compaignie
Of heuene and to al holy chirche, allas!   30
To longe haast thow bathid in þat folie.
Ryse vp and pourge thee of thy trespas.

Seynt Austyn seith, whiles a man abydith
In heresie or scisme and list nat flee
Therfro, his soule fro God he diuidith   35
And may nat saued been in no degree.
For what man holdith nat the vnitee
Of holy chirche, neithir his bapteeme
Ne his almesse, how large þat it be,
To helthe him profyte ne God qweeme.   40

And yit moreouer he seith thus also,
Thogh þat an heretyk for Crystes name
Shede his blood and his lyf for Cryst forgo,
Shal nat him saue. Allas, the harm and shame.
May nat thy smert thy sturdy herte attame?   45
Obeie, obeie in the name of Ihesu.
Thow art of merit and of honur lame;
Conquere hem two and thee arme in vertu.

If thyn hy herte, bolnynge in errour,
To holy chirche can nat buxum be,   50
Beholde Theodosius emperour,
How humble and buxum vnto God was he.
No reward took he of his dignitee,
But as a lamb to holy chirche obeide.
In the scripture may men rede and se   55
How meekly of the bisshop grace he preide.

Th'offense which þat he ageyn God wroghte
Was nat so greet as thyn, by many fold,
And yit ful heuy he was and it forthoghte,
Obeyyng as þat holy chirche hath wold.   60
Thow þat thy soule to the feend haast sold,
Bye it agayn thurgh thyn obedience.
Thyn heresie is al to hoor and old.
Correcte thee at Crystes reuerence.

And for thy soules helthe do eek so.   65
Thy pryde qwenche and thy presumpcioun.
Wher thow hast been to Crystes feith a fo,
Plante in thyn herte a deep contricioun
And hennesfoorth be Crystes champioun.
The welle of mercy renneth al in brede,   70
Drynke therof syn ther is swich foysoun;
Thyn hertes botel therof fille, I rede.

Thow haast offendid God wondirly sore,
And nathelees, if thow the wilt amende,
Thogh thy gilt wer a thousande tymes more,   75
Axe him mercy and He wole it thee sende.
Thow art vnwys thogh thow thee wys pretende,
And so been alle of thyn opinioun.
To God and holy chirche thow thee bende.
Caste out thy venym thurgh confessioun.   80

Thow seist, confessioun auriculeer
Ther needith noon, but it is the contrarie;
Thow lookist mis, thy sighte is nothyng cleer.
Holy writ therin is thyn aduersarie,
And clerkes alle fro thy conceit varie   85
Þat Crystes partie holden and maynteene.
Leue þat conceit, lest þat thow miscarie.
Waar of the swerd of God for it is keene.

Heere in this lyf vnto God mercy crie,
And with the ax or hamer of penance   90
Smyte on the stoon, slee thyn obstinacie.
Haue of thy synnes heuy remembrance.
Rowne in the preestes ere, and the greuance
Of thy soule meekly to him confesse.
And in the wal of heuene, is no doutance,   95
Thow shalt a qwik stoon be for thy goodnesse.

Oldcastel, how hath the feend thee blent!
Where is thy knyghtly herte? Art thow his thral?
Thow errest foule eek in the sacrament
Of the auter, but how in special   100
For to declare it needith nat at al;
It knowen is in many a regioun.
Now syn the feend hath youen the a fal.
Qwyte him, let see, ryse vp and slynge him doun.

Ryse vp a manly knyght out of the slow   105
Of heresie. O lurkere as a wrecche,
Whereas thow erred haast, correcte it now.
By humblesse thow mayst to mercy strecche;
To holy chirche go and there fecche
The holsum oyle of absolucion.   110

75 thousande] M^l.

If thow of soules hurt ne shame recche,
Thow leesist heuene and al knyghtly renoun.

Par cas, thow to thyself shame it arettist
Vnto prelatz of holy chirche obeie.
If it be so, thy conceit thow missettist;   115
What man aright can in his herte weye
The trouthe of that? To Ihesu Cryst, I seye,
Princypally is þat obedience.
God hath ordeyned preestes to purueye
Salue of penance for mannes offense.

Vnto seint Petir and his successours
And so foorth doun God hath His power lent.
Go to the preest, correcte thyn errours,
With herte contryt vnto God ybent.
Despute no more of the sacrament.   125
As holy chirche biddith, folwe it.
And hennesforward, as by myn assent,
Presume nat so mochil of thy wit.

I putte cas, a prelat or a preest
Him viciously gouerne in his lyuynge,   130
Thow oghtist reewe on it whan thow it seest
And folwe him nat; but aftir his techynge
Thow oghtest do, and for thyn obeyynge
Thow shalt be sauf; and if he teche amis
Toform God shal he yeue a rekenynge,   135
And þat astreit, the greet peril is his.

Lete holy chirche medle of the doctryne
Of Crystes lawes and of his byleeue,
And lete alle othir folk therto enclyne
And of our feith noon argumentes meeue.   140
For if we mighte our feith by reson preeue,
We sholde no meryt of our feith haue.
But nowadayes a baillif or reeue
Or man of craft wole in it dote or raue.

Somme wommen eek, thogh hir wit be thynne,   145
Wole argumentes make in holy writ.
Lewed calates, sittith down and spynne
And kakele of sumwhat elles, for your wit
Is al to feeble to despute of it.

To clerkes grete apparteneth þat aart;   150
The knowleche of þat God hath fro yow shit;
Stynte and leue of, for right sclendre is your paart.

Oure fadres olde and modres lyued wel
And taghte hir children as hemself taght were
Of holy chirche, and axid nat a del   155
'Why stant this word heere? and why this word there?
Why spak God thus, and seith thus elleswhere?
Why dide he this wyse, and mighte han do thus? '
Our fadres medled nothyng of swich gere.
þat oghte been a good mirour to vs.   160

If land to thee be falle of heritage
Which þat thy fadir heeld in reste and pees
With title iust and treewe in al his age,
And his fadir before him brygelees,
And his and his and so foorth, doutelees,
I am ful seur who so wolde it thee reue,
Thow woldest thee deffende and putte in prees.
Thy right thow woldest nat, thy thankes, leue.

Right so, where as our goode fadres olde
Possessid were and hadden the seisyne   170
Peisible of Crystes feith, and no man wolde
Inpugne hir right, it sit vs to enclyne
Therto, let vs no ferthere ymagyne
But as þat they dide, occupie our right
And in oure hertes fully determyne
Our title good, and keepe it with our might.

Who so hath right and nat wole it deffende,
It is no manhode, it is cowardyse.
And as in this cas he shal God offende
So greuously þat he shal nat souffyse   180
The maugree for to bere in no wyse
Fro Cryst þat right first greew. And if þat we
Nat shuln susteene it, we been ful vnwyse.
Himself is feith, right, trouthe, and al bontee.

The cristen emperour Iustinian,
As it is writen, who so list it see,
Made a lawe deffendyng euery man,
Of what condicion or what degree

Þat he were of, nat sholde hardy be
For to despute of the feith openly;   190
And there vpon sundry peynes sette he
Þat peril sholde eschued be therby.

Bewar, Oldcastel, and for Crystes sake
Clymbe no more in holy writ so hie.
Rede the storie of Lancelot de Lake,
Or Vegece, *Of the aart of chiualrie*,
The *Seege of Troie* or *Thebes*. Thee applie
To thyng Þat may to th'ordre of knyght longe.
To thy correccioun now haaste and hie,
For thow haast been out of ioynt al to longe.   200

If thee list thyng rede of auctoritee,
To thise stories sit it thee to goon,
To *Iudicum*, *Regum* and *Iosue*,
To *Iudith*, and to *Paralipomenon*,
And *Machabe*. And as sikir as stoon,
If Þat thee list in hem bayte thyn ye,
More autentik thing shalt thow fynde noon
Ne more pertinent to chiualrie.

Knyghtes so dide in tymes Þat be past
Whan they had tendrenesse of hire office.   210
In Crystes feith they stooden stidefast.
And as Þat the preest, hir soules norice,
Hem goostly fedde and yaf hem the notice
Of Crystes lore, with obedience
They took it. But now regneth swich malice
That buxumnesse is put in abstinence.

O Constantyn, thow prince of hy nobleye,
O Cristen emperour whos worthynesse
Desdeyned nat to holy chirche obeye
But didest al thy peyne and bisynesse   220
With wel disposid spirit of meeknesse
The ministres of God for to honure,
How thow wroghtist hast thow so strong witnesse
That lyue it shal whil the world wole endure.

Thow took nat on thee hir correccioun,
Ne vpon hem thow yaf no iugement,
Swich was to God thy good affeccioun.

Thow seidest: 'They been goddes to vs sent.
And þat it is nothyng conuenient
That a man sholde goddes iuge and deeme.'   230
Thow were a noble and a worthy regent.
Wel was byset on thee thy diadeeme.

Blessid be God, fro whom deryued is
Al grace, our lige lord which þat is now
Our feithful Cristen prince and kyng, in this
Folwith thy steppes. O, for shame, thow
Oldcastel, thow haast longe tyme ynow
Folwed the feend. That thow no lenger do,
Do by my reed, it shal be for thy prow.
Flee fro the feend, folwe tho princes two.   240

Reward had and consideracioun
Vnto the dignitees of tho persones,
Thow art of a scars reputacioun.
A froward herte haast thow for the nones.
Bowe and correcte thee, come of at ones.
Foule haast thow lost thy tyme many a day.
For thyn vnfeith men maken many mones.
To God retourne and with his feith dwelle ay.

Thogh God thee haue souffrid regne a whyle,
Be nat to bold, bewar of his vengeance.   250
He tarieth for thow sholdist reconsyle
Thee to him and leue thy mescreaunce.
Holsum to thee now were a variaunce
Fro the feend to our lord God and fro vice
Vnto vertu, þat were his hy plesaunce
And his modres, mankyndes mediatrice.

Some of thy fetheres weren plukkid late,
And mo shuln be. Thow shalt it nat asterte.
Thow art nat wys ageyn God to debate.
The flood of pryde caste out of thyn herte.   260
Grace is alyue, to God thee conuerte.
Thow maist been his if thee list him obeie.
If thow nat wilt so, sorrer shalt thow smerte
Than herte of man may thynke or tonge seye.

238 That] thogh

Almighty God, thow lord of al and syre,
Withouten whom is no goodnesse wroght,
This knyght of thyn habundant grace enspyre.
Remembre how deere þat thow haast him boght.
He is thyn handwerk, lord, refuse him noght
Thogh he thee haue agilt outrageously.   270
Thow þat for mercy deidest, change his thoght.
Benigne lord, enable him to mercy.

Yee þat peruerted him, yee folk dampnable,
Yee heretikes þat han him betrayed
That manly was, worthy and honurable,
Or þat he hadde of your venym assayed.
I doute it nat, your wages shal be payed
Sharply but yee correcte your trespas.
In your fals errour shul yee been outrayed
And been enhabited with Sathanas.   280

Yee, with your sly coloured argumentes
Which þat contenen nothyng but falshode,
Han in this knyght put so feendly ententes
Þat he is ouercharged with the lode
Which yee han leid on his good old knyghthode,
That now a wrecchid knyght men calle may.
The lak of feith hath qwenchid his manhode.
His force ageyn God naght is at assay.

Prynce of preestes our lige lord yee calle
In scorn, but it is a style of honour.   290
Auctoritee of preest excedith alle
Eerthely powers, thogh it seeme sour
To the taast of your detestable errour.
They þat in the feith been constaunt and sad
In seint Petres wordes han good fauour
And fayn been to fullfille þat he bad.

All eerthely princes and othir men
Bysshops to obeie commandid he.
Yee han no ground to holde ther ayen.
Spirituel thynges passe in dignitee   300
Alle the thynges temporel þat be,
As moche as dooth the soule the body.
In the scriptures serche and yee shul see
Þat it no lees at al is hardily.

Two lightes God made in the firmament
Of heuene. A more made he and a lesse.
The gretter light to the day hath he lent
It for to serue in his cleer brightnesse.
The smaller to the nyght in soothfastnesse
He lente also to helpe it with his light.   310
Two dignitees they toknen in liknesse,
Auctoritee papal and kynges might.

Looke how moche and how greet dyuersitee
Betwixt the sonne ther is and the moone;
So moche is a popes auctoritee
Aboue a kynges might. Good is to doone
Þat yee aryse out of your errour soone
Þat therein walwid han, goon is ful yore.
And but yee do, God I byseeche a boone,
Þat in the fyr yee feele may the sore.   320

Yee þat nat sette by preestes power,
Crystes rebels and foos men may you calle.
Yee waden in presumpcioun to fer.
Your soules to the feend yee foule thralle.
Yee seyn: 'A preest in deedly synne fall,
If he so go to messe, he may not make
Crystes body.' Falsly yee erren alle
Þat holden so. To deepe yee ransake.

As wel may a preest þat is vicious
Þat precious body make day by day   330
As may a preest þat is ful vertuous.
But waar the preest, his soule it hurte may
And shal, but he be cleene, it is no nay.
Be what he be, the preest is instrument
Of God, thurgh whos wordes trustith this ay.
The preest makith the blessid sacrament.

Yee medle of al thyng, yee moot shoo the goos.
How knowen yee what lyf a man is ynne?
Your fals conceites renne aboute loos.
If a preest synful be and fro God twynne,   340
Thurgh penitence he may ageyn God wynne.
No wight may cleerly knowen it or gesse
Þat any preest, beynge in deedly synne,
For awe of God dar to the messe him dresse.

Yee seyn also: 'Ther sholde be no pope,
But he the beste preest were vpon lyue.'
O, wherto graspen yee so fer and grope
Aftir swich thyng? Yee mowe it neuere dryue
To the knowleche. Nothyng thereof stryue.
Medle nat therwith, let al swich thyng passe.   350
For if þat yee do, shul yee neuere thryue.
Yee been therin as lewde as is an asse.

Many man outward seemeth wondir good
And inward is he wondir fer therfro.
No man be iuge of þat but he be wood.
To God longith þat knowleche and no mo.
Thogh he be right synful, sooth is also
The hy power þat is to him committid
As large as Petres is, it is right so.
Amonges feithful folk, this is admittid.   360

What, is the lawe the werse of nature
If þat a iuge vse it nat aright?
No thyng, God wot, auyse him þat the cure
Therof hath take, looke he do but right.
Waar þat he nat stonde in his owne light.
Good is þat he his soule keepe and saue.
Your fals conceites puttith to the flight,
I rede, and Crystes mercy axe and haue.

Yee þat pretenden folwers for to be
Of Crystes disciples nat lyue sholde   370
Aftir the flesshly lustes, as doon yee
Þat rekken nat whos wyf yee take and holde.
Swich lyf the disciples nat lyue wolde,
For cursid is the synne of aduoutrie.
But yee therin so hardy been and bolde
Þat yee no synne it holden ne folie.

If yee so holy been as yee witnesse
Of your self, thanne in Crystes feith abyde.
The disciples of Cryst had hardynesse
For to appeere. They nat wolde hem hyde   380
For fere of deeth, but in his cause dyde.
They fledden nat to halkes ne to hernes
As yee doon þat holden the feendes syde,
Whiche arn of dirknesse the lanternes.

Ne neuere they in forcible maneere
With wepnes roos to slee folk and assaille
As yee diden late in this contree heere,
Ageyn the kyng stryf to rere and bataille.
Blessid be God, of your purpos yee faille,
And faille shuln. Yee shuln nat foorth therwith.   390
Yee broken meynee, yee wrecchid rascaille
Been al to weyk, yee han therto no pith.

Also yee holden ageyn pilgrimages,
Whiche arn ful goode if þat folk wel hem vse,
And eek ageyns the makynge of ymages.
What, al is nat worth þat yee clappe and muse.
How can yee by reson yourself excuse
Þat yee nat erren, whan yee folk excite
To vice and stire hem vertu to refuse?
Waar Goddes strook, it peisith nat a lyte.   400

For to visite seintes is vertu
If þat it doon be for deuocioun.
And elles, good is be therof eschu.
Meede wirkith in good entencioun.
Be cleene of lyf and be in orisoun.
Of synne talke nat in thy viage.
Let vertu gyde thee fro toun to toun.
And so to man profitith pilgrimage.

And to holde ageyn ymages makynge,
Be they maad in entaille or in peynture,   410
Is greet errour. For they yeuen stirynge
Of thoghtes goode and causen men honure
The seint after whom maad is that figure,
And nat worsshipe it, how gay it be wroght.
For this knowith wel euery creature
Þat reson hath, þat a seint is it noght.

Right as a spectacle helpith feeble sighte
Whan a man on the book redith or writ
And causith him to see bet than he mighte,
In which spectacle his sighte nat abit   420
But gooth thurgh and on the book restith it;
The same may men of ymages seye.
Thogh the ymage nat the seint be, yit
The sighte vs myngith to the seint to preye.

Ageyn possessions yee holden eek
Of holy chirche, and that is eek errour.
Your inward ye is ful of smoke and reek.
While heere on eerthe was our sauueour,
Whom angels diden seruice and honour,
Purses had he. Why? For his chirche sholde   430
So haue eek aftir, as seith mine auctour.
Yee goon al mis, al is wrong þat yee holde.

Iustinian emperour had swich cheertee
To holy chirche, as þat seith the scripture,
Þat of goodes how large or greet plentee
It hadde of yifte of any creature,
Him thoghte it youe in the best mesure
Þat mighte been, his herte it loued so.
Yee neuere yaf hem good, perauenture.
What title han yee aght for to take hem fro?   440

And if yee had aght youe hem or this tyme,
Standynge in the feith as yee oghten stonde,
Sholden they now for your charge and your cryme
Despoillid been of þat they haue in honde?
Nay, þat no skile is. Yee shul vndirstonde
They nyght and day labouren in prayeere
For hem that so yaf. Styntith and not fonde
To do so, for first boght wole it be deere.

Presumpcion of wit and ydilnesse
And couetyse of good, tho vices three   450
Been cause of al your ydil bysynesse.
Yee seyn eek: 'Goodes commune oghten be.'
Þat ment is in tyme of necessitee,
But nat by violence or by maistrie
My good to take of me or I of thee,
For þat is verray wrong and robberie.

If þat a man the soothe telle shal,
How þat your hertes in this cas been set,
For to ryfle is your entente final.
Yee han be bisy longe aboute a net   460
And fayn wolde han it in the watir wet
The fissh to take, which yee han purposid.
But God and our lord lige hath yow let.
It nis ne shal been as yee han supposid.

Men seyn: 'Yee purpose hastily appeere
The worm for to sleen in the pesecod.'
Come on whan yow list, yee shul reewe it deere.
The feend is your cheef, and oure heed is God.
Thogh we had in oure handes but a clod
Of eerthe, at your heedes to slynge or caste   470
Were wepne ynow or a smal twig or rod.
The feith of Cryst stikith in vs so faste.

We dreden nat, we han greet auantage
Whethir we lyue or elles slayn be we
In Crystes feith. For vp to heuenes stage,
If we so die, our soules lift shul be.
And on þat othir part yee feendes, yee
In the dirk halke of hell shul descende.
And yit with vs abit this charitee,
Our desir is þat yee yow wolde amende.   480

Yee holden many anothir errour mo
Then may be writen in a litil space,
But lak of leisir me commandith ho.
Almighty God byseeche I of his grace
Enable yow to seen his blessid face,
Which þat is o God and persones three.
Remembre yow, heuene is a miry place
And helle is full of sharp aduersitee.

Yit, Oldcastel, for him þat his blood shadde
Vpon the crois, to his feith torne agayn.   490
Forgete nat the loue he to vs hadde,
Þat blisful lord þat for alle vs was slayn.
From hennesforward trouble nat thy brayn,
As thow hast doon, ageyn the feith ful sore.
Cryst of thy soule glad be wolde and fayn.
Retourne knyghtly now vnto his lore.

Repente thee and with him make accord.
Conquere meryt and honour, let see.
Looke how our cristen prince, our lige lord,
With many a lord and knyght beyond the see   500

Laboure in armes. And thow hydest thee
And darst nat come and shewe thy visage.
O fy, for shame! How can a knyght be
Out of th'onur of this rial viage?

Sum tyme was no knyghtly turn nowhere
Ne no manhode shewid in no wyse
But Oldcastel wolde, his thankes, be there.
How hath the cursid fiend changid thy gyse!
Flee from him and all his wirkes despyse.
And þat ydoon, vnto our cristen kyng   510
Thee hie as faste as þat thow canst dyuyse
And humble eek thee to him for anythyng.   Cest tout.

THE COMPLAINT OF HOCCLEVE

Aftir þat heruest inned had hise sheues,
And that the broun sesoun of Mihelmesse
Was come, and gan the trees robbe of her leues
That grene had ben and in lusty freisshenesse,
And hem into colour of ȝelownesse
Had died and doun throwen vndir foote,
That chaunge sanke into myn herte roote.

For freisshly brouȝte it to my remembraunce
That stablenesse in this worlde is ther noon.
Ther is no þing but chaunge and variaunce.   10
Howe welthi a man be or wel begoon,
Endure it shal not, he shal it forgoon.
Deeth vndir foote shal him þriste adoun.
That is euery wiȝtes conclucioun,

Wiche for to weyue is in no mannes myȝt,
Howe riche he be, stronge, lusty, freissh, and gay.
And in the ende of Nouembre vppon a niȝt,
Siȝynge sore as I in my bed lay
For this and oþir þouȝtis wiche many a day
Byforne I tooke, sleep cam noȯn in myn ye,   20
So vexid me the þouȝtful maladie.

I sy wel sithin I with siknesse last
Was scourgid, cloudy hath bene þe fauour
That shoon on me ful briȝt in times past.
The sunne abated and þe dirke shour
Hilded doun riȝt on me and in langour
Me made swymme, so that my spirite
To lyue no lust had ne no delite.

The greef aboute myn herte so swal
And bolned euere to and to so sore,   30

2 broun] C brome   3 gan] L gon   6 throwen] C threste
12 C *omits line*   12 not] Y he not   17 a] Y *om.*
22 sithin] C *om.*   26 and] Y *om.*   28 no lust] C in lust
28 ne no] B nor nokyns LY ne nokynnes
29 so] S *adds* sore *above line*   30 bolned] C volued   30 so] C *om.*

That nedis oute I muste therwithal.
I thouȝte I nolde kepe it cloos no more,
Ne lete it in me for to eelde and hore.
And for to preue I cam of a womman,
I braste oute on þe morwe and þus bigan.

Here endith my prolog and folwith my compleinte

Almyȝty God, as liketh his goodnesse,
Vesiteþ folke al day as men may se
With los of good and bodily sikenesse,
And amonge othir he forȝat not me.
Witnesse vppon the wilde infirmite   40
Wiche þat I hadde, as many a man wel knewe,
And wiche me oute of my silfe caste and threwe.

It was so knowen to þe peple and kouthe
That counseil was it noon ne not be miȝt.
Howe it wiþ me stood was in euery mannes mouþe,
And þat ful sore my frendis affriȝt.
They for myn helþe pilgrimages hiȝt
And souȝte hem, somme on hors and somme on foote —
God ȝelde it hem — to gete me my boote.

But al þouȝ the substaunce of my memorie   50
Wente to pleie as for a certein space,
Ȝit the lorde of vertue, the kyng of glorie,
Of his hiȝe myȝt and his benigne grace
Made it for to retourne into the place
Whens it cam, wiche at Alle Halwemesse
Was fiue ȝeere, neither more no lesse.

And euere sithin, thankid be God oure lord
Of his good and gracious reconsiliacioun,
My wit and I haue bene of suche acord
As we were or the alteracioun   60
Of it was. But by my sauacioun,

43 kouthe] Y kuothe   44 not] C *om.*   47 helþe] B hele
47 pilgrimages] S pilgimages   48 somme[1]] C *om.*   49 it] C *om.*
50 al þouȝ] C though all   53 his[2]] BCLY *om.*   55 Whens] C Thens
55 at] BCLY was at   55 Alle] C *om.*   56 ȝeere] Y ȝer seth
61 Of] C Or   61 by] BLY be

Sith þat time haue I be sore sette on fire
And lyued in greet turment and martire.

For þou3 that my wit were hoom come a3ein,
Men wolde it not so vndirstonde or take.
With me to dele hadden they disdein.
A rietous persone I was and forsake.
Min oolde frendshipe was al ouershake.
No wi3t with me list make daliaunce.
The worlde me made a straunge countinaunce,   70

Wich þat myn herte sore gan to tourment.
For ofte whanne I in Westmynstir Halle
And eke in Londoun amonge the prees went,
I sy the chere abaten and apalle
Of hem þat weren wonte me for to calle
To companie. Her heed they caste awry
Whanne I hem mette, as they not me sy.

As seide is in þe sauter, mi3t I sey,
They þat me sy fledden awey fro me.
For3eten I was, al oute of mynde, awey,   80
As he þat deed was from hertis cherte.
To a lost vessel lickned mi3te I be.
For manie a wi3t aboute me dwelling
Herde I me blame and putte in dispreisyng.

Thus spake manie oone and seide by me,
'Al þou3 from him his siiknesse sauage
Withdrawen and passed as for a time be,
Resorte it wole, namely in suche age
As he is of.' and thanne my visage
Bigan to glowe for the woo and fere.   90
Tho wordis, hem vnwar, cam to myn eere.

'Whanne passinge hete is,' quod þei, 'trustiþ this,
Assaile him wole a3ein that maladie.'

62 Sith] S written over erasure BCLY om.   63 greet] B om.
69 wi3t] B om.   69 make] C to make BLY add me.
70 straunge] BLY strong   71 Wich] SBLY With
71 sore gan to] C gan sore   72 ofte] L om.
74-146 L lacks next folio   75 weren] C was
80 awey] BY allweye   88 wole] C adds and
93 him wole a3ein] C ayenne wolle hym

And ȝit, parde, thei token hem amis.
Noon effecte at al took her prophecie.
Manie someris bene past sithen remedie
Of that God of his grace me purueide.
Thankid be God, it shoop not as þei seide.

What falle shal, what men so deme or gesse,
To him that woot euery hertis secree   100
Reserued is. It is a lewidnesse,
Men wiser hem pretende þan thei be.
And no wiȝt knowith, be it he or she,
Whom, howe, ne whanne God wole him vesite.
It happith ofte whanne men wene it lite.

Somtime I wende as lite as any man
For to han falle into that wildenesse.
But God whanne him liste may, wole, and can
Helthe withdrawe and sende a wiȝt siiknesse.
Thouȝ man be wel this day, no sikernesse   110
To hym behiȝte is that it shal endure.
God hurte nowe can and nowe hele and cure.

He suffrith longe but at the laste he smit.
Whanne þat a man is in prosperite,
To drede a falle comynge it is a wit.
Who so that taketh hede ofte may se
This worldis chaunge and mutabilite.
In sondry wise howe nedith not expresse.
To my mater streite wole I me dresse.

Men seiden I loked as a wilde steer,   120
And so my looke aboute I gan to throwe.
Min heed to hie, anothir seide, I beer;
'Ful bukkissh is his brayn, wel may I trowe.'
And seide the thridde — and apt is in þe rowe
To site of hem that a resounles reed
Can ȝeue — 'no sadnesse is in his heed.'

94 token hem] C tolden her tale   99 What] BY That
99 men so] B so men   100 hertis] B mannes   secree] B secrete Y seree
104 him] BC hym   105 it] C om.   107 that] C om.
111 To] Y So   115 a²] Y om.   118 howe] C it
120 steer] B starre   121 looke] Y booke   throwe] B thowe
125 hem] C om.   a] C om.   126 he added above can   is] BY om.

Chaunged had I my pas, somme seiden eke,
For here and there forþe stirte I as a roo,
Noon abood, noon areest, but al brainseke.
Another spake and of me seide also,   130
My feet weren ay wauynge to and fro
Whanne þat I stonde shulde and wiþ men talke,
And þat myn yen souȝten euery halke.

I leide an eere ay to as I by wente
And herde al. And þus in myn herte I caste;
'Of longe abidinge here I may me repente,
Lest that of hastinesse I at the laste
Answere amys; beste is hens hie faste,
For if I in þis prees amys me gye,
To harme wole it me turne and to folie.'   140

And this I demed wel and knewe wel eke,
What so þat euere I shulde answere or seie
They wolden not han holde it worth a leke.
Forwhy, as I had lost my tunges keie
Kepte I me cloos and trussid me my weie,
Droupinge and heuy and al woo bistaad.
Smal cause hadde I, me þouȝte, to be glad.

My spirites labouriden euere ful bisily
To peinte countenaunce, chere, and look,
For þat men spake of me so wondringly,   150
And for the verry shame and feer I qwook.
Thouȝ myn herte hadde be dippid in þe brook
It weet and moist was ynow of my swoot,
Wiche was nowe frosty colde, nowe firy hoot.

And in my chaumbre at home whanne þat I was,
Mysilfe aloone I in þis wise wrouȝt.

128 I] Y om.   my] me   129 abood noon areest] C areste none abode
130 spake and] C om.   131 wauynge] BY wadyng
134 ay to] C to ay   135 And²] B om.   136 me] Y om.
137 that] Y it   138 amys] B of mys   is hens hie] C I hie hens
140 To] Y Tho   141 this] C þus   144 lost] C lefft
148 spirites] BLY add hem   euere ful] written over erasure BLY þen
ful C om.   149 and] Y Ad   150 wondringly] BCLY wondirly
152 þe] L a Y om.
153 moist was ynow] ynow above line BCLY mosty inow was (Y was now)
154 colde] C adds and   155 þat] C om.   156 aloone] Y A lonḡ

I streite vnto my mirrour and my glas
To loke howe þat me of my chere þouȝt,
If any othir were it than it ouȝt.
For fain wolde I if it not had bene riȝt　　　　160
Amendid it to my kunnynge and myȝt.

Many a saute made I to this mirrour,
Thinking if þat I looke in þis manere
Amonge folke as I nowe do, noon errour
Of suspecte look may in my face appere.
This countinaunce, I am sure, and þis chere
If I it forthe vse is no thing repreuable
To hem þat han conceitis resonable.

And therwithal I þouȝte þus anoon:
'Men in her owne cas bene blinde al day,　　　170
As I haue herde seie manie a day agoon,
And in þat same plite I stonde may.
Howe shal I do? Wiche is the beste way
My troublid spirit for to bringe in rest?
If I wiste howe, fain wolde I do the best.'

Sithen I recouered was, haue I ful ofte
Cause had of anger and inpacience,
Where I borne haue it esily and softe,
Suffringe wronge be done to me and offence,
And not answerid aȝen but kepte scilence,　～　180
Leste þat men of me deme wolde and sein,
'Se howe this man is fallen in aȝein.'

As that I oones fro Westminstir cam
Vexid ful greuously with þouȝtful hete,
Thus thouȝte I: 'a greet fool I am
This pauyment adaies thus to bete
And in and oute laboure faste and swete,
Wondringe and heuinesse to purchace,
Sithen I stonde out of al fauour and grace.'

157 streite] BLY sterte　　158 howe] C on chere] LY *add* me
160 not had] BCLY had not　riȝt] C ariht
161 Amendid] C Amende　　162 this] C þ^t　　171 a day] Y days
174 troublid] C troublie　　175 do] C do for
177 inpacience] Y paciencie　　185 a] BLY *om.*　fool] L foly
186 pauyment] C pament

And thane þou3te I on þat othir side: 190
'If that I not be sen amonge þe prees,
Men deme wole that I myn heed hide
And am werse than I am, it is no lees.'
O lorde, so my spirit was restelees.
I sou3te reste and I not it fonde,
But ay was trouble redy at myn honde.

I may not lette a man to ymagine
For aboue þe mone if þat him liste.
Therby the sothe he may not determine,
But by the preef ben thingis knowen and wiste.   200
Many a doom is wrappid in the myste.
Man bi hise dedis and not by hise lookes
Shal knowen be, as it is writen in bookes.

Bi taaste of fruit men may wel wite and knowe
What that it is. Othir preef is ther noon.
Euery man woote wel that, as þat I trowe.
Ri3t so thei that deemen my wit is goon,
As 3it this day ther deemeth many oon
I am not wel, may as I by hem goo
Taaste and assay if it be so or noo.   210

Vppon a look is harde men hem to grounde
What a man is; therby the sothe is hid.
Whethir hise wittis seek bene or sounde
By countynaunce is it not wist ne kid.
Thou3 a man harde haue oones been bitid,
God shilde it shulde on him contynue alway.
By commvnynge is the beste assay.

I mene to commvne of thingis mene,
For I am but ri3t lewide douteles
And ignoraunt. My kunnynge is ful lene.   220
3it homely resoun knowe I neuerethelees.
Not hope I founden be so resounlees

191 not be] C am not   193 than] Y and
198 Fer] BLY Ferrere   aboue] C about   þat] C om.
199 not] above line   200 ben] C by   201 B om. line
205 is] Y as   209 may] C many   212 is therby] C therby is
215 harde haue oones] C ones harde   been] B om.
216 on him contynue] B contynu on hym   217 By] BLY add gode
222 hope I founden be] C I hope to be founden

As men deemen. Marie, Crist forbede!
I can no more. Preue may the dede.

If a man oones falle in drunkenesse,
Shal he contynue therynne euere mo?
Nay. Þouȝ a man do in drinking excesse
So ferforþe þat not speke he ne can ne goo
And hise wittis wel ny bene refte him fro
And buried in the cuppe, he aftirward   230
Cometh to hymsilfe aȝein. Ellis were it hard.

Riȝt so, þouȝ þat my witte were a pilgrim
And wente fer from home, he cam aȝain.
God me deuoided of the greuous venim
That had enfectid and wildid my brain.
See howe the curteise leche most souerain
Vnto the seke ȝeueth medicine
In nede and hym releueth of his greuous pine.

Now lat this passe. God woot many a man
Semeth ful wiis by countenaunce and chere   240
Wiche, and he tastid were what he can,
Men miȝten licken him to a fooles peere.
And som man lokeþ in foltisshe manere,
As to þe outwarde doom and iugement,
That at þe preef discreet is and prudent.

But algatis howe so be my countinaunce,
Debaat is nowe noon bitwixe me and my wit,
Al þouȝ þat ther were a disseueraunce
As for a time bitwixe me and it.
The gretter harme is myn, þat neuere ȝit   250
Was I wel lettrid, prudent, and discreet.
Ther neuere stood ȝit wiis man on my feet.

The sothe is this. Suche conceit as I had
And vndirstonding, al were it but smal,

224 may] LY *add* men   225 oones falle] C falle ones
226 euere] C in euere   228 not speke he ne] C he nat speke
228 þouȝ] Y thoght   234 deuoided] BCLY voidid
235 wildid] B wilkyd   238 greuous] C *om.*   243 in] C in a
245 and] BLY *add* right   248 Al] As þouȝ] B those B those þat] B thos
249 As for a] C Afore

Bifore þat my wittis weren vnsad,
Thanked be oure lorde Ihesu Crist of al,
Suche haue I nowe. But blowe is ny oueral
The reuerse, wher þoruȝ moche is my mornynge
Wiche causeth me thus syȝe in compleinynge.

Sithen my good fortune hath chaungid hir chere,   260
Hie tyme is me to crepe into my graue.
To lyue ioielees, what do I here?
I in myn herte can no gladnesse haue.
I may but smal seie but if men deme I raue.
Sithen oþir þing þan woo may I noon gripe,
Vnto my sepulcre am I nowe ripe.

My wele adieu, farwel my good fortune.
Oute of ȝoure tables me planed han ȝe.
Sithen wel ny eny wiȝt for to commvne
With me loth is, farwel prosperite.   270
I am no lenger of ȝoure liuere.
ȝe haue me putte oute of ȝoure retenaunce.
Adieu my good aeunture and good chaunce.

And aswithe aftir thus biþouȝte I me:
'If þat I in this wise me dispeire,
It is purchas of more aduersite.
What nedith it my feble wit appeire
Sith God hath made myn helþe home repeire?
Blessid be he. And what men deme and speke
Suffre it, þenke I, and me not on me wreke.'   280

But somdel had I reioisinge amonge
And a gladnesse also in my spirite,
That thouȝ þe peple took hem mis and wronge,
Me deemyng of my siiknesse not quite,
ȝit for they compleined the heuy plite
That they had seen me in wiþ tendirnesse
Of hertis cherte, my greef was the lesse.

258 þoruȝ] C for   259 syȝe] BLY sey C her'   261 me] C to me
264 I] C þᵗ I   if] C om.
266-7 C ffor ioie is ther none yit vn to me ripe/Setheñ othir thinge
than woo may I none gripe   267 my] C om.
273 and] C adds my Y Ad   275 me] B om.
278 Sith] CY Sithen   home] C adds to
279 and] BCLY or   helþe] Y helpe
283 thouȝ] Y thoght   mis] Y om.

In hem putte I no defaute but oon;
That I was hool þei not ne deme kowde.
And day be day þei sye me bi hem goon   290
In hete and coolde, and neiþer stille or lowde
Knewe þei me do suspectly. A dirke clowde
Hir siȝt obscurid withynne and wiþoute,
And for al þat were ay in suche a doute.

Axide han they ful ofte sithe and freined
Of my felawis of the Priue Seel,
And preied hem to telle hem wiþ herte vnfeined
Howe it stood with me, wethir yuel or wel.
And they the sothe tolde hem euery del,
But þei helden her wordis not but lees.   300
Thei miȝten as wel haue holden her pees.

This troubly liif hath al to longe endurid.
Not haue I wist hou in my skyn to tourne.
But nowe mysilfe to mysilfe haue ensurid
For no suche wondringe aftir this to mourne.
As longe as my liif shal in me soiourne
Of suche ymaginynge I not ne recche.
Lat hem deeme as hem list and speke and drecche.

This othir day a lamentacioun
Of a wooful man in a book I sy,   310
To whom wordis of consolacioun
Resoun ȝaf spekynge effectuelly,
And wel esid myn herte was therby.
For whane I had a while in þe book reed
With the speche of Resoun was I wel feed.

The heuy man, wooful and angwisshous,
Compleined in þis wise and þus seide he:
'My liif is vnto me ful encomborus,
For whidre or vnto what place I flee
My wickidnessis euere folowen me.   320

---

289 ne] BCLY me   291 or] Y ne   293 and] BCLY add eke
294 ay] C thay   295 sithe] Y sithis   297 hem] C om.
298 wethir] C wher   301 margin Hic est lamentacio hominis dolentis
304 to mysilfe haue] LY have to myself   haue] C is
309 margin Anima mea augustiis est cor meum fluctuat vbi/cumque
fugero mala mea sequitur me sicut vm/bra persequitur corpus et non
possum ea fugere   318 encomborus] Y encomerous

As men may se the shadwe a body sue,
And in no manere I may hem eschewe.

'Vexacioun of spirit and turment
Lacke I riȝt noon. I haue of hem plente.
Wondirly bittir is my taast and sent.
Woo be þe time of my natiuite!
Vnhappi man, that euere shulde I be!
O deeth, thi strook a salue is of swetnesse
To hem þat lyuen in suche wrecchidnesse.

'Gretter plesaunce were it me to die   330
By manie foolde than for to lyue so.
Sorwes so manie in me multiplie
That my liif is to me a verre foo.
Comforted may I not be of my woo,
Of my distresse see noon ende I can.
No force howe soone I stinte to be a man.'

Thanne spake Resoun: 'What meneth al this fare?
Thouȝ welþe be not frendly to thee, ȝit
Oute of thin herte voide woo and care.'
'By what skile, howe, and by what reed and wit,'   340
Seide this wooful man, 'miȝte I doon it? '
'Wrastle,' quod Resoun, 'aȝein heuynesse
Of þe worlde, troublis, suffringe, and duresse.

'Biholde howe many a man suffrith dissese   •
As greet as þou, and al away grettere,
And þouȝ it hem pinche sharply and sese,
ȝit paciently thei it suffre and bere.
Thinke hereon, and the lesse it shal þe dere.
Suche suffraunce is of mannes gilte clensinge
And hem enableth to ioie euere lastinge.   350

324 riȝt] C om.   326 BLY om. line   þe] S be   327 I] BCLY it
328 thi] LY þi   329 margin O mors quam dulcis male viuentibus
330 margin Melius est me mori quam infeliciter viuere
334 I] B om.   335 see . . . . can] C none eende see I ne can
341 miȝte] B I myght
343 troublis suffringe] BLY sufferyng trowblis   duresse] S duresses
345 al away] BY all way   346 it hem pinche] C hym it punsshe
347 ȝit] BLY They   350 hem] BCY hym   350 euere] B euery

'Woo, heuinesse, and tribulacioun
Comen aren to me[n] alle and profitable.
Thouȝ greuous be mannes temptacioun,
It sleeth man not. To hem þat ben suffrable
And to whom Goddis strook is acceptable
Purueied ioie is, for God woundith tho
That he ordeined hath to blis to goo.

'Golde purgid is, thou seest, in þe furneis·
For þe finer and clenner it shal be.
Of þi dissese the weiȝte and þe peis   360
Bere liȝtly, for God to prove þe
Scourgid þe hath wiþ sharpe aduersite;
Not grucche and seie "Whi susteine I this?"
For if þou do, thou the takist amis.

'But þus þou shuldist þinke in þin herte
And seie to þee: "Lorde God, I haue a gilte
So sore I moot for myn offensis smerte
As I am worthi. O lorde, I am spilte
But þou to me þi mercy graunte wilte.
I am ful sure þou maist it not denie.   370
Lorde, I me repente and I the mercy crie." '

Lenger I þouȝte reed haue in þis book,
But so it shope þat I ne miȝte nauȝt.
He þat it ouȝte aȝen it to him took,
Me of his hast vnwar. Ȝit haue I cauȝt
Sum of the doctrine by Resoun tauȝt
To þe man, as above haue I said.
Wel þerof I holde me ful wel apaid.

For euere sithen sett haue I the lesse
By the peples ymaginacioun,   380

351 *margin* Dolor tristicia communa sunt omnibus. Hic/deus
vulnerat eos quos preparat ad eternam salutem   352 men] SBCLY me
352 and profitable] B unprofitable
354 sleeth] Y fleth   hem] Y hẙm
358 *margin* Aurum de quoquitur purgatur in fornace ut/purius fiat
et cetera is] B as   359 shal] BLY shulde   360 and] C and eke
363 Not] S *holed*   364 the takist] C takest the   365 þin] C priue
367 sore] C *adds* that   moot] BLY not   370 maist] C wolt
372 reed haue] C to haue radde
373 it] C *om.*   nuaȝt] BY no aghte L noaght
378 Wel þerof] BCLY Wherof

Talkinge this and þat of my siknesse
Wich cam of Goddis visitacioun.
Miȝte I haue be founde in probacioun
Not grucching but han take it in souffraunce,
Holsum and wiis had be my gouernaunce.

Farwel my sorwe! I caste it to the cok.
With pacience I hensforþe thinke vnpike
Of suche þoutȝtful dissese and woo the lok
And lete hem out þat han me made to sike.
Hereafter oure lorde God may if him like   390
Make al myn oolde affeccioun resorte,
And in hope of þat wole I me comforte.

Thoruȝ Goddis iust doom and his iugement
And for my best, nowe I take and deeme,
ȝaf þat good lorde me my punischement.
In welthe I tooke of him noon hede or ȝeme
Him for to plese and him honoure and queme,
And he me ȝaf a boon on for to gnawe
Me to correcte and of him to have awe.

He ȝaf me wit and he tooke it away   400
Whane that he sy that I it mis dispente,
And ȝaf aȝein whane it was to his pay.
He grauntide me my giltis to repente
And hensforwarde to sette myn entente
Vnto his deitee to do plesaunce
And to amende my sinful gouernaunce.

Laude and honour and þanke vnto þee be,
Lorde God that salue art to al heuinesse,
Thanke of my welthe and myn aduersitee,
Thanke of myn elde and of my seeknesse,   410
And thanke be to thin infinit goodnesse
And thi ȝiftis and benefices alle,
And vnto thi mercy and grace I calle.

387 I hensforþe] C hensforthe I
389 han me] BL me haue   Y have   me made] C made me
394 I take] C take I   395 ȝaf] C Of   396 In] B And in
402 his] C hym   404 forwarde] C forth
405 deitee] C dignete   do] C doo hym   411 to] L om.
412 And] BCLY For   and] BCLY and thy

THE DIALOGUE WITH A FRIEND

A Tribute to Humphrey, Duke of Gloucester

'And of o thyng now wel I me remembre
Why thow purposist in this book trauaille.
I trowe þat in the monthe of Septembre
Now last, or nat fer from, it is no faille —
No force of the tyme, it shal nat auaille   530
To my mateere, ne it hyndre or lette —
Thow seidist of a book thow were in dette

'Vnto my lord þat now is lieutenant,
My lord of Gloucestre, is it nat so? '
'Yis soothly, freend, and as by couenant
He sholde han had it many a day ago.
But seeknesse and vnlust and othir mo
Han be the causes of impediment.'
'Thomas, than this book haast thow to him ment? '

'Yee sikir, freend, ful treewe is your deemynge.   540
For him it is þat I this book shal make.
As blyue as þat I herde of his comynge
Fro France I penne and ynke gan to take
And my spirit I made to awake,
Þat longe lurkid hath in ydilnesse
For any swich labour or bisynesse.

'But of sum othir thyng fayn trete I wolde,
My noble lordes herte with to glade,
As therto bownden am I deepe and holde.
On swich mateere, by God þat me made,   550
Wolde I bestowe many a balade,
Wiste I what. Good freend, telle on what is best
Me for to make, and folwe it am I prest.

'Next our lord lige, our kyng victorious,
In al this wyde world lord is ther noon
Vnto me so good ne so gracious,
And haath been swich yeeres ful many oon.
God yilde it him. As sad as any stoon

His herte set is and nat change can
Fro me, his humble seruant and his man.   560

'For him I thoghte han translated Vegece
Which tretith of the art of chiualrie.
But I see his knyghthode so encrece
Þat nothyng my labour sholde edifie,
For he þat art wel can for the maistrie.
Beyonde, he preeued hath his worthynesse,
And among othre Chirburgh to witnesse.

'This worthy prynce lay before þat hold,
Which was ful strong, at seege many a day,
And thens for to departe hath he nat wold   570
But knyghtly there abood vpon his pray
Til he by force it wan, it is no nay.
Duc Henri, þat so worthy was and good,
Folwith this prince, as wel in deede as blood.

'Or he to Chirburgh cam in iourneyynge,
Of Constantyn he wan the cloos and yle,
For which laude and honur and hy preysynge
Rewarden him and qwyten him his whyle.
Thogh he beforn þat had a worthy style,
Yit of noble renoun is þat encrees.   580
He is a famous prince, doutelees.

'For to reherce or telle in special
Euery act þat his swerd in steel wroot there
And many a place elles, I woot nat al,
And thogh euery act come had to myn ere,
T'exepresse hem my spirit wolde han fere
Lest I his thank par chaunce mighte abregge
Thurgh vnkonnynge if I hem sholde allegge.

'But this I seye. He callid is Humfrey
Conueniently, as þat it seemeth me,   590
For this conceit is in myn herte alwey.
Bataillous Mars in his natiuitee
Vnto þat name of verray specialtee
Titled him, makynge him therby promesse
Þat strecche he sholde into hy worthynesse.

586 T'exepresse] To xepresse

'For Humfrey, as vnto myn intellect,
Man make I shal in Englissh is to seye.
And þat byheeste hath taken treewe effect,
As the commune fame can bywreye.
Whoso his worthy knyghthode can weye   600
Duely in his conceites balaunce
Ynow hath wherof his renoun enhaunce.

'To cronicle his actes were a good deede,
For they ensaumple mighte and encorage
Ful many a man for to taken heede
How for to gouerne hem in the vsage
Of armes. It is a greet auauntage
A man before him to haue a mirour
Therin to see the path vnto honour.

'O lord, whan he cam to the seege of Roon   610
Fro Chirburgh, whethir fere or cowardyse
So ny the walles made him for to goon
Of the town as he dide? I nat souffyse
To telle yow in how knyghtly a wyse
He logged him there and how worthyly
He baar him. What! he is al knyght, soothly.

'Now good freend, shoue at the cart, I yow preye.
What thyng may I make vnto his plesance?
Withouten your reed noot I what to seye.'
'O no, pardee, Thomas, O no, ascance.'   620
'No, certein, freend, as now no cheuissance
Can I. Your conseil is to me holsum.
As I truste in yow, mynystreth me sum.'

The Friend's Advice

He a long tyme in a studie stood,
And aftir þat thus tolde he his entente.   660
'Thomas, sauf bettre auys, I holde it good,
Syn now the holy seson is of lente
In which it sit euery man him repente
Of his offense and of his wikkidnesse,
Be heuy of thy gilt and the confesse

'And satisfaccion do thow for it.
Thow woost wel, on wommen greet wyt and lak

Ofte haast thow put. Be waar lest thow be qwit.
Thy wordes fille wolde a quarter sak,
Which thow in whyt depeynted haast with blak.   670
In hir repreef mochil thyng haast thow write,
That they nat foryeue haue ne foryite.

'Sumwhat now wryte in honour and preysynge
Of hem. So maist thow do correccioun
Sumdel of thyn offense and misberynge.
Thow art cleene out of hire affeccioun.
Now syn it is in thyn eleccioun
Whethir thee list hir loue ageyn purchace
Or stonde as thow doost out of loue and grace,

'Be war, rede I, cheese the bettre part.   680
Truste wel this, wommen been fell and wyse.
Hem for to plese lyth greet craft and art.
Wher no fyr maad is, may no smoke aryse.
But thow haast ofte, if thow thee wel auyse,
Maad smoky brondes. And for al þat gilt
Yit maist thow stonde in grace, if þat thow wilt.

'By buxum herte and by submissioun
To hir graces yildinge thee coupable,
Thow pardon maist haue and remissioun
And do vnto hem plesance greable.   690
To make partie art thow nothyng able.
Humble thy goost, be nat sturdy of herte.
Bettre than thow art han they maad to smerte.

'The Wyf of Bathe take I for auctrice
Þat wommen han no ioie ne deyntee
Þat men sholde vpon hem putte any vice.
I woot wel so, or lyk to þat, seith shee.
By wordes writen, Thomas, yilde thee.
Euene as thow by scripture hem haast offendid,
Right so let it be by wrytynge amendid.'   700

'Freend, thogh I do so, what lust or pleisir
Shal my lord haue in þat? Noon, thynkith me.'
'Yis, Thomas, yis. His lust and his desir
Is, as it wel sit to his hy degree,
For his desport and mirthe in honestee

With ladyes to haue daliance,
And this book wole he shewen hem, par chance.

'And syn he thy good lord is, he be may
For thee swich mene þat the lightlyere
Shuln they foryeue thee. Putte in assay   710
My conseil, let see, nat shal it thee dere.
So wolde I doon if in thy plyt I were
Leye hond on thy breest, if thow wilt so do
Or leue. I can no more seyn therto.'

THE TALE OF JONATHAS

Whilom an emperour prudent and wys
Regned in Rome and hadde sones three,
Whiche he hadde in greet chiertee and greet prys.
And whan it shoop so þat th'infirmitee
Of deeth, which no wight may eschue or flee,
Him threew doun in his bed, he leet do call   90
His sones and before him they cam all.

And to the firste he seide in this maneere:
'Al th'eritage which at the dyynge
Of my fadir he me lefte, al in feere
Leue Y thee. And al þat of my byynge
Was with my peny, al my purchacynge,
My second sone, byqwethe Y to thee.'
And to the thirde sone thus seide he:

'Vnmeeble good right noon, withouten ooth,
Thee yeue Y may. But Y to thee dyuyse   100
Iewelles three — a ryng, brooch, and a clooth —
With whiche, and thow be gyed as the wyse,
Thow maist gete al þat oghte thee souffyse.
Who so þat the ryng vsith for to were
Of alle folk the loue he shal conquere.

'And who so the brooch berith on his brest,
It is eek of swich vertu and swich kynde
That thynke vpon what thyng him lykith best,
And he as blyue shal it haue and fynde.
My wordes, sone, enprynte wel in mynde.   110
The clooth eek hath a meruillous nature
Which þat committed shal be to thy cure.

'And who so sit on it, if he wishe where
In al the world to been, he sodeynly
Withoute more labour shal be there.
Sone, tho three iewelles byqwethe Y
To thee, vnto this effect certeynly
Þat to the studie of the vniuersitee
Thow go, and þat Y bidde and charge thee.'

Whan he had thus seid, the vexacioun   120
Of deeth so haastid him þat his spiryt
Anoon forsook his habitacioun
In his body. Deeth wolde no respyt
Him yeue at al. He was of his lyf qwyt,
And biried was with swich solempnitee
As fil to his imperial dignitee.

Of the yongeste sone I telle shal
And speke no more of his brethren two,
For with hem haue Y nat to do at al.
Thus spak the modir Ionathas vnto: 130
'Syn God his wil hath of thy fadir do,
To thy fadres wil wole Y me confourme
And trewely his testament parfourme.

'He three iewelles, as thow knowist weel,
A ryng, a brooch, and a clooth, thee byqweeth,
Whos vertues he thee tolde euery deel
Or þat he paste hens and yald vp the breeth.
O goode God, his departynge, his deeth
Ful greuously stikith vnto myn herte.
But souffred moot been al, how sore it smerte.'   140

In þat cas wommen han swich heuynesse
Þat it nat lyth in my konnynge aright
Yow telle of so greet sorwe the excesse.
But wyse wommen konne take it light,
And in short whyle putte vnto the flight
Al sorwe and wo and cacche ageyn confort.
Now to my tale make Y my resort.

'Thy fadres wil, my sone, as Y seide eer,
Wole Y parfourme. Haue heer the ryng and go
To studie anoon, and whan þat thow art theer,   150
As thy fadir thee bad, do euene so.
And as thow wilt, my blessyng haue also.'
Shee vnto him as swythe took the ryng
And bad him keepe it weel for anythyng.

He wente vnto the studie general
Wher he gat loue ynow and aqueyntance
Right good and freendly, the ryng causynge al.
And on a day to him befil this chance.

With a womman, a morsel of plesance,
By the streetes of the vniuersitee   160
As he was in his walkynge mette he.

And right as blyue he with hire had a tale,
And therwithal sore in hir loue he brente.
Gay, freesh, and pykid was shee to the sale,
For to þat ende and to þat entente
Shee thidir cam. And bothe foorth they wente,
And he a pistle rowned in hir ere.
Nat woot Y what, for Y ne cam nat there.

Shee was his paramour, shortley to seye.
This man to folkes all was so leef   170
Þat they him yaf habundance of moneye.
He feestid folk and stood at hy boncheef.
Of the lak of good he felte no greef
Al whyles þat the ryng he with him hadde.
But faylynge it, his frendshipe gan sadde.

His paramour, which þat ycallid was
Fellicula, meruailled right greetly
Of the despenses of this Ionathas,
Syn shee no peny at al with him sy.
And on a nyght as þat shee lay him by   180
In the bed, thus shee to him spak and seide,
And this peticion assoill him preyde:

'O reuerent sire, vnto whom', quod shee,
'Obeye Y wole ay with hertes humblesse,
Syn þat yee han had my virginitee,
Yow Y byseeche of your hy gentillesse,
Tellith me whens comth the good and richesse
That yee with feesten folk and han no stoor
By aght Y see can, ne gold ne tresor.'

'If Y telle it,' quod he, 'parauenture   190
Thow wilt deskeuere it and out it publisshe.
Swich is wommannes inconstant nature
They can nat keepe conseil worth a risshe.
Bettre is my tonge keepe than to wisshe
Þat Y had kept cloos þat is goon at large,
And repentance is thyng þat Y moot charge.'

'Nay, goode sire, haldith me nat suspect.
Doutith nothyng, Y can be right secree.
Wel worthy wer it me to been abiect
From al good conpaignie if Y', quod shee,   200
'Vnto yow sholde so mistake me.
Beeth nat adrad your conseil me to shewe.'
'Wel,' seide he, 'thus it is at wordes fewe.

'My fadir, the ryng which þat thow maist see
On my fyngir, me at his dyyng day
Byqweeth, which this vertu and propretee
Hath, þat the loue of men he shal haue ay
Þat werith it. And ther shal be no nay
Of what thyng þat him lykith axe and craue,
But with good wil he shal as blyue it haue.   210

'Thurgh þat rynges vertuous excellence
Thus am Y ryche and haue euere ynow.'
'Now sire, yit a word by your licence
Suffrith me for to seye and speke now.
Is it wysdam, as þat it seemeth yow,
Were it on your fyngir continuelly? '
'What woldest thow mene,' quod he, 'therby?

'What peril therof mighte ther befall? '
'Right greet,' quod shee, 'as yee in conpaignye
Walke often, fro your fyngir mighte it fall   220
Or plukkid of been in a ragerie
And so be lost, and þat were folie.
Take it me, let me been of it wardeyn,
For as my lyf keepe it wole Y certeyn.'

This Ionathas, this innocent yong man,
Yeuynge vnto hir wordes ful credence,
As youthe nat auysed best be can,
The ryng hir took of his insipience.
Whan this was doon, the hete and the feruence
Of loue þat he had beforn purchaced   230
Was qweynt and loues knotte was vnlaced.

Men of hir yiftes for to stynte gan.
'A,' thoghte he, 'for the ryng Y nat ne bere,
Faillith my loue. Fecche me, womman,'
Seide he, 'my ryng anoon, Y wole it wer.'

Shee roos and into chambre dressith her,
And whan shee therein hadde been a whyle,
'Allas,' quod shee, 'out on falshode and gyle!

'The chiste is broken, and the ryng take out.'
And whan he herde hir conplaynte and cry,   240
He was astoned sore and made a shout
And seide, 'Cursid be þat day þat Y
The mette first or with myn yen sy.'
She wepte and shewid outward cheer of wo,
But in hir herte was it nothyng so.

The ryng was sauf ynow and in hir cheste
It was. Al þat shee seide was lesyng,
As sum womman othir whyle atte beste
Can lye and weepe whan is hir lykyng.
This man sy hir wo and seide, 'Derlyng,   250
Weepe no more. Goddes help is ny.'
To him vnwist how fals shee was and sly.

He twynned thens and hoom to his contree
Vnto his modir the streight way he wente.
And whan shee sy thidir comen was he,
'My sone,' quod shee, 'what was thyn entente
Thee fro the scoole now for to absente?
What causid thee fro scoole hidir to hye?'
'Modir, right this,' seide he, 'nat wole Y lye.

'For soothe, modir, my ryng is ago.   260
My paramour to keepe Y betook it,
And it is lost, for which Y am ful wo.
Sorwefully vnto myn herte it sit.'
'Sone, often haue Y warned thee, and yit
For thy profyt Y warne thee, my sone.
Vnhonest wommen thow heereaftir shone.

'Thy brooch anoon right wole Y to thee fette.'
Shee broghte it him and charged him ful deepe,
Whan he it took and on his brest it sette,
Bet than he dide his ryng he sholde it keepe,   270
Lest he the los bewaille sholde and weepe.
To the vniuersitee, shortly to seyn,
In what he kowde he haastid him ageyn.

And whan he comen was, his paramour
Him mette anoon, and vnto hire him took
As þat he dide erst, this yong reuelour.
Hir conpaignie he nat a deel forsook
Thogh he cause hadde, but as with the hook
Of hir sleighte he beforn was caght and hent,
Right so he was deceyued eft and blent.　　　　280

And as thurgh vertu of the ryng before
Of good he hadde habundance and plentee
While it was with him or he hadde it lore,
Right so thurgh vertu of the brooch had he
What good him list. Shee thoghte, 'How may this be?
Sum pryuee thyng now causith this richesse
As dide the ryng heer before, Y gesse.'

Wondrynge heeron, shee preide him and besoghte
Bysyly nyght and day þat telle he wolde
The cause of this. But he anothir thoghte;　　　　290
He mente it cloos for him it kept be sholde.
And a long tyme it was or he it tolde.
Shee kepte ay to and to and seide, 'Allas,
The tyme and hour þat euere Y bore was!

'Truste yee nat on me, sire? ' she seide.
'Leuer me were be slayn in this place
By þat good lord þat for vs all deide
Than purpose ageyn yow any fallace.
Vnto yow wole Y be, my lyues space,
As treewe as any womman in eerthe is　　　　300
Vnto a man. Doutith nothyng of this.'

Smal may shee do þat can nat wel byheete,
Thogh nat parfourmed be swich a promesse.
This Ionathas thoghte hir wordes so sweete
Þat he was dronke of the plesant swetnesse
Of hem. And of his foolissh tendrenesse
Thus vnto hire he spak and seide tho:
'Be of good confort. Why weepist thow so?'

And shee therto answerde thus sobbynge:
'Sire,' quod shee, 'myn heuynesse and dreede　　　　310
Is this. Y am adrad of the leesynge
Of your brooch, as almighty God forbeede

It happid so.' 'Now what, so God thee speede,'
Seide he, 'woldist thow in this cas consaille?'
Quod shee, 'Þat Y keepe mighte it, sanz faille.'

He seide, 'Y haue a fere and dreede algate,
If Y so dide, thow woldest it leese,
As thow lostist my ryng, now goon but late.'
'First, God preye Y.' quod shee, 'þat Y nat cheese
But þat myn herte as the cold frost may freese,   320
Or elles be it brent with wylde fyr.
Nay, seurly it to keepe is my desyr.'

To hir wordes credence he yaf pleneer
And the brooch took hire. And aftir anoon,
Whereas he was beforn ful leef and cheer
To folk and hadde good, al was agoon.
Good and frendshipe him lakkid, ther was noon.
'Womman, me fecche the brooch,' quod he, 'swythe.
Into thy chambre for it go. Now hy the!'

Shee into chambre wente as þat he bad,   330
But she nat broghte þat he sente hir fore.
Shee mente it nat. But as shee had be mad,
Hir clothes hath shee al torent and tore
And cryde, 'Allas, the brooch away is bore!
For which Y wole anoon right with my knyf
Myself slee. Y am weery of my lyf.'

This noyse he herde, and blyue he to hire ran
Weenynge shee wolde han doon as shee spak.
And the knyf in al haaste þat he can
From hire took and threew it behynde his bak,   340
And seide: 'For the los ne for the lak
Of the brooch sorwe nat. Y foryeue al.
I truste in God þat yit vs helpe he shal.'

To th'emperice his modir this young man
Ageyn him dressith. He wente hire vnto,
And whan shee sy him, shee to wondre gan.
Shee thoghte, 'Now sumwhat ther is misdo,'
And seide: 'Y dreede thy iewelles two
Been lost now, per cas the brooch with the ryng.'
'Modir,' he seide, 'yee, by heuene kyng.'   350

'Sone, thow woost wel no iewel is left
Vnto thee now but the clooth precious,
Which Y thee take, thee chargynge eft
The conpaignie of wommen riotous
Thow flee, lest it be to thee so greuous
That thow it nat susteene shalt ne bere.
Swich conpaignie, on my blessyng, forbere.'

The clooth shee fette, and it hath him take.
And of his lady his modir his leeue
He took, but first this forward gan he make.   360
'Modir,' seide he, 'trustith this weel, and leeue
Þat Y shal seyn for sooth yee shul it preeue.
If Y leese this clooth, neuere Y your face
Hensfoorth se wole ne yow preye of grace.

'With Goddes help Y shal do wel ynow.'
Hir blessyng he took and to studie is go.
And as beforn told haue Y vnto yow,
His paramour, his priuee mortel fo,
Was wont for to meete him, right euene so
Shee dide thanne and made him plesant cheere.   370
They clippe and kisse and walke homward in feere.

Whan they were entred in the hows, he spradde
This clooth vpon the ground and theron sit
And bad his paramour, this womman badde,
To sitte also by him adoun on it.
Shee dooth as þat he commandith and bit.
Had shee his thoght and vertu of the clooth
Wist, to han sete on it had shee been looth.

Shee for a whyle was ful sore affesid.
This Ionathas wisshe in his herte gan: 380
'Wolde God þat Y mighte thus been esid,
That as on this clooth Y and this womman
Sitte here, as fer were as þat neuere man
Or this cam.' And vnnethe had he so thoght
But they with the clooth thidir weren broght

Right to the worldes ende, as þat it were.
Whan apparceyued had shee this, shee cryde
As thogh shee thurgh girt had be with a spere.
'Harrow, allas þat euere shoop this tyde!

How cam we hidir? ' 'Nay,' he seide, 'abyde, 390
Wers is comynge. Heer soul wole Y thee leue.
Wylde beestes thee shuln deuoure or eue,

'For thow my ryng and brooch haast fro me holden.'
'O reuerent sire, haue vpon me pitee,'
Quod shee. 'If yee this grace do me wolden,
As me brynge hoom ageyn to the citee
Whereas Y this day was, but if þat yee
Hem haue ageyn, of foul deeth do me dye.
Your bontee on me kythe, Y mercy crye.'

This Ionathas kowde nothyng be waar, 400
Ne take ensample of the deceites tweyne
Þat shee dide him beforn, but feith hir baar.
And hire he comanded on dethes peyne
Fro swiche offenses thensfoorth hir restreyne.
Shee swoor and made therto foreward.
But herkneth how shee baar hire aftirward.

Whan shee sy and kneew þat the wratthe and ire
Þat he to hire had born was goon and past
And al was wel, shee thoghte him eft to fyre.
In hir malice ay stood shee stidefast, 410
And to enquere of him was nat agast,
In so short tyme how þat it mighte be
That they cam thidir out of hir contree.

'Swich vertu hath this clooth on which we sitte,'
Seide he, 'þat where in this world vs be list,
Sodeynly with the thoght shuln thidir flitte,
And how thidir come vnto vs vnwist
As thyng fro fer vnknowen in the mist.'
And therwith to this womman fraudulent,
'To sleepe', he seide, 'haue I good talent. 420

'Let see,' quod he, 'strecche out anoon thy lappe,
In which wole I myn heed doun leye and reste.'
So was it doon, and he anoon gan nappe.
Nappe? Nay, he sleep right wel atte beste.
What dooth this womman, oon the fikileste

402 hir] him

Of wommen all, but þat clooth þat lay
Vndir him shee drow lyte and lyte away.

Whan shee it had al, 'Wolde God,' quod shee,
'I were as I was this day morwenynge.'
And therwith this roote of iniquitee   430
Had hir wissh and soul lefte him ther slepynge.
O Ionathas, lyk to thy perisshynge
Art thow. Thy paramour maad hath thy berd.
Whan thow wakist, cause hast thow to be ferd.

But thow shalt do ful wel, thow shalt obteene
Victorie on hire. Thow haast doon sum deede
Plesant to thy modir, wel can I weene,
For which our lord God qwyte shal thy meede
And thee deliure out of thy woful dreede.
The chyld whom þat the modir vsith blesse,   440
Ful often sythe is esid in distresse.

Whan he awook and neithir he ne fond
Womman ne clooth, he wepte bittirly
And seide: 'Allas, now is ther in no lond
Man werse, I trowe, begoon, than am Y!'
On euery syde his look he caste and sy
Nothyng but briddes in the eir fleynge
And wylde beestes aboute him rennynge,

Of whos sighte he ful sore was agrysid.
He thoghte: 'Al this wel disserued Y haue.   450
What eilid me to be so euel auysid,
That my conseil kowde I nat keepe and saue?
Who can fool pleye, who can madde or raue,
But he þat to a womman his secree
Deskeuereth — the smert cleueth now on me.'

COMMENTARY

The Complaint of the Virgin (before 1405)

Like all Hoccleve's minor verse in this selection except the three *rondeaux* which come from Huntington MS HM 744, this poem occurs in Huntington MS HM 111. But the initial leaf containing the first six stanzas is lost. The poem also occurs as one of fourteen inset in an English prose version of Deguileville's *Pèlerinage de l'âme* in British Library MS Egerton 615, made in 1413 (in some later copies dated 1400 by error) perhaps for Joan FitzAlan, countess of Hereford (d.1419), Henry V's maternal grandmother and an early patron of Hoccleve; and the missing stanzas are based on that text. These poems are printed by Furnivall as an appendix (pp. xxiii–lxii) to his edition of the *Regiment*, and their possible attribution to Hoccleve is discussed above, pp.xiv–xv. Six of these lyrics recur in a Carthusian miscellany, British Library MS Additional 37049, *c.*1450, described in 'The English manuscripts of *Mandeville's Travels'*, *Transactions of the Edinburgh Bibliographical Society* iv (1966), 203–6, and in a Victoria MS (p.xv, above).

Deguileville's verse at this point, like its English translation, has more matter, which Hoccleve clearly omitted if his final *Cest tout* is to be credited. It seems that an enterprising translator borrowed and expanded Hoccleve's poem to fit its original context. Such practice would be unremarkable; in his verse translation of Deguileville's *Pèlerinage de la vie humaine* Lydgate planned to include Chaucer's *ABC to the Virgin* in its original context. It is, of course, possible that Hoccleve is the translator of the *Pèlerinage de l'âme*.

The *Complaint of the Virgin* is a close translation of Deguileville's lyric, made at the request of the countess of Hereford probably very early in Hoccleve's poetic career. For a modern taste the lyric is full of incongruity and of excessive length. But the central drama of the Cross, and especially the *stabat mater dolorosa* theme, inspired the most common type of medieval verse, and this dramatic, as it were eye-witness record of the Virgin's lament is, at very least, no worse than most. Like the early Chaucer, Hoccleve follows his source (British Library MS Additional 22937, fos. 108–9^V) attentively, but in the process of recasting the French octosyllabics into English rhyme royal he adds much of his own, e.g. the successful pathos of lines 39–42. He shows a command of rhyme and metre but not always of syntax, which sometimes reads awkwardly. On the other hand, his sentences are not rigidly bound by the metrical line or even the stanzaic mould and sometimes have an idiomatic fluency of their own, pleasantly free from line-filling tags and taking Deguileville's rhetorical flourishes in their stride. These virtues and defects are present in all Hoccleve's verse.

11 *Have*: the plain infinitive form without the preposition *to* is used after some auxiliary verbs and in certain other contexts, cf. 54, 66, and the second *Balade to Sir Henry Somer* 6, the first *Balade to King Henry V* 16, the *Complaint of Hoccleve* 187, the *Regiment of Princes* 1971, etc. See J. Kerkhof, *Studies in the language of Chaucer* (1966), pp. 49–60.

by the lappe: the common ME collocation is 'to catch by the lap', i.e. to take hold of, as in *Troilus* ii. 448, and probably suggested to Hoccleve the use of *caught* in line 12.

18 *shadwist*: the metaphor derives from Luke 1:35, *et virtus altissimi obumbrabit tibi*. In similar contexts the word is rendered *obumbrid* (Lydgate, *Balade to Our Lady* 102) and *enoumbre* (*Mandeville's Travels*, ed. M. C. Seymour (1967) p.1). Deguileville has *obumbras*.

36 Luke 1:41.

43 Luke 11:27.

50 Luke 2:35.

125 *Come of*: an idiomatic phrase implying a strong command, borrowed from falconry or hunting. Cf. *Troilus* ii.1738.

133 *with wrong*: 'falsely'. A literal translation of *par tort*. Cf. 'Mandeville' and the story of the girl accused of adultery, ed. cit. 50/31.

139 Genesis 9:23.

163 *anothir*: i.e. St. John, to whom Jesus on the Cross entrusted Mary, John 19:26.

183 *Mara*: a play on the French *amère* 'bitter', cf. Latin *amara*, which a literal translation (as Chaucer's *ABC to the Virgin* 50), obscures. Hoccleve was doubtless familiar with Exodus 15:23 and the hebraism *Marah* there explained.

221 Cf. *Troilus* ii.811. The sudden alternations of temperature, characteristic of fever and love-sickness, are called *accesse*.

223 *steerelees*: 'rudderless', cf. Chaucer's *Complaint to his Purse* 12. Like *brydillees* (*La Male Regle* 78), the adjective is first recorded in Hoccleve, and is probably modelled on Chaucer's *recchelees* and *waterlees* (the *General Prologue* 179–180).

243–5 Hoccleve alters the sense of his French source, presumably to make a neat ending to his translation which he does not require to match Deguileville's lines:

> Et son escorce hors percier
> Pour vous faire son ius succier.
> Venez quar ma pomme foraige
> Est mise a partuy saige.

In its original context the lyric is, in the rubric of MS Egerton 615, f.63, 'a lamentacioun of the grene tree, complaynyng of the losyng of hire appill'.

The Mother of God (before 1405)

This title, given to the poem by Thynne in 1532 who ascribed it to Chaucer and attached to the poem until its rejection from the Chaucer canon in 1866, is preferred to Hoccleve's rubric *Ad beatam virginem*, which he also uses for another lyric. There is no note of origin in the manuscript, and the poem was probably an uncommissioned religious poetic exercise, perhaps in imitation of Chaucer's *ABC to the Virgin*. The intense personal note of *brennyng leccherie* in line 27 and elsewhere does not seem relevant to the Hoccleve of *La Male Regle*, and the way the poet passes from the particular *me* to the general *us* is equally uncharacteristic. Probably the theme of lechery is merely the antithesis of Mary's chastity, heavily emphasized here as in all medieval verse, and Hoccleve is closely following a French source, as in the *Complaint of the Virgin* which, in tone and sentiment, this poem closely resembles.

As in his three shorter Marian lyrics in Huntington Library MS 744, the simple dignity and rhythms give the poem an air of sustained sanctity, unlike Lydgate's Marian lyrics, which are much more aureate in diction and seem at times more like exercises in literary ingenuity than genuine prayer.

20 Cf. Daniel 5:27.

26 *grace and favour*: the phrase was in origin probably a double translation (in the common manner of the time) of *gratia*, cf. *favour and grace* in the *Clerk's Tale* 102 and Hoccleve's *Complaint* 189.

27 *brennyng leccherie*: the description may reflect St. Paul, I Corinthians 7:9, *melius est enim nubare quam uri*, or it may look forward to the flames of hell, cf. the *Parson's Tale*, *de luxuria*: 'Seint Iohn seith that avowtiers shullen been in helle, in a stank brennynge of fyr and of brymston.' In either case the original force was probably lost. In *La Male Regle*, written when he was about 35, Hoccleve confesses his ignorance of *loues aart* 153, and the phrase is perhaps inherited from the French source postulated above. However, as a patient but disappointed suppliant for a benefice he may have known the *temptacioun. . . of wikkid thoght*, and it may be relevant that the *Regiment* 1555–764 discusses marriage and its variations at length, although such discussion is a medieval literary convention.

35 *wikkid thoght*: the context certainly gives this phrase a sexual connotation, which it could in any case bear. But in the *Regiment* 7, 13, etc. *thoght* means 'care, anxiety', and Hoccleve frequently speaks of a near-suicidal despair.

77 *yee*: i.e. Christ and Mary. In this poem *yee* is always plural. Elsewhere (e.g. *Balades to Sir Henry Somer*) the form is used as a respectful singular.

105 *Crystes derlyng*: a common English collocation for St. John at least as old as Ælfric (d. 1020), ultimately reflecting John 13:23.

106 *heuenely gemmes tweyne*: probably a conscious echo of the *gemini*, the heavenly twins of the zodiac.

108 *bysy peyne*: the phrase possibly derives from Chaucer's *Balade to Truth* 108.

La Male Regle De T. Hoccleue (1405)

If this poem had a literary model, it was more likely a contemporary French or English composition than one of the classical or post-classical hymns to the goddess of health; Miss E. Thornley, 'The Middle English Penitential Lyric and Hoccleve's Autobiographical Poetry', *Neuphilologische Mitteilungen* lxviii (1967), argues that it belongs to the tradition of the penitential lyric, of which it is a parody. Its immediate origin may be a genuine response to a personal illness, though whether this was more than a severe hangover, aggravated by an achingly empty purse, seems doubtful. In 1405, when he wrote the poem (as the references in lines 417-23 indicate), Hoccleve was about 35 and unmarried, and no doubt looked backward at youth's follies with regret and forward at his future prospects with distaste. But at such a vantage point, he manages, whether deliberately or not, to convey a sympathetic and balanced tone which attests a still unbroken spirit, and even in learning of his desperate need of coin, the reader is aware that he lacks the means to continue his misrule. Perhaps the final stanzas which appeal for payment of his annuity were a late addition, prompted by news of the lord Furnivall's appointment, to a poem already complete. Certainly, the undoubted success of the device of using himself as poetic material in the Chaucerian manner pointed the way to his later verse.

The core of the poem yields valuable information on the London of his day as well as unexpected delight, in both respects comparable to the near-contemporary anonymous balade *London Lickpenny*. The most convenient account of fifteenth-century London, with a useful end-map, occurs in C.J. Kingsford, *Prejudice and Promise in fifteenth-century England* (1925, reissued 1962). See also M.B. Honeybourne, *A Sketch Map of London under Richard II*, London Topographical Society Publication 93 (1960); S. Thrupp, *The Merchant Class of Medieval London* (1968); D.W. Robertson, *Chaucer's London* (1968); G. Mathew, *The Court of Richard II* (1968). The poem is also edited, with useful notes, by E.P. Hammond, *English Verse between Chaucer and Surrey* (1927), pp. 60-6, 402-4.

1-8 The apostrophes to *Helthe*, with the supporting rhetorical question and description in this and the following stanzas, are conventional. But Hoccleve easily and refreshingly sheds the more cumbersome literary devices and effects a natural beginning.

23 'now I can distinguish between a feast-day and a fast-day'.

25 *smert cotidian*: 'a recurring sickness', cf. *tertidian* 'a fever which recurs every other day'. *cotidian* is here an adjective 'daily' qualifying the noun *smert*, cf. line 40. See Bartholomaeus Anglicus, *De proprietatibus rerum* vii. 38 and Trevisa's translation, *On the Properties of Things* (1975), i.386.

28 *fruyt*: 'wisdom', a common metaphor, used by Chaucer (e.g. *Squire's Tale* 74, *Nun's Priest's Tale* 623) and others to indicate the 'sentence' of a book, and derived from the rhetoric manuals. The metaphor is developed in line 64.

39 Despite the alliteration, cf. line 221, the line has a distinctly Chauce-
rian ring.

50 *in cheef*: a metaphor from land tenure *in capite*, which the tenant
held directly from the feudal lord to whom he owed allegiance. Cf.
modE 'chief-rent'.

64 *chyldly sapience*: 'imperfect knowledge', 'wisdom of a young man',
cf. *Troilus* iv. 804 and the *Regiment* 2058.

67 *Regnynge which*: 'during which time'. The construction is based on
the Latin ablative absolute, possibly directly on an administrative phrase
like *regnante Henrico*. Cf. the *Complaint* 91 and 375 and Chaucer's use
of *during* in the *Legend of Good Women* 283, and *OED* sub *during* and
failing.

78 *brydillees*: first recorded occurrence. Cf. note to the *Complaint of
the Virgin* 223.

83 *rakil*: of obscure origin, the word is recorded from 1300 in the sense
'hasty, rash, coarse'. Hoccleve probably echoes Chaucer (*Troilus* iii.429,
Manciple's Tale 185 and 235).

95 *so rype vnto my pit*: 'so near to death'. The idea recurs in Hoccleve's
Complaint 266, the *Regiment* 952.

111 *twenty*: a round number, generally used without specific intent. Cf.
Squire's Tale 43, 320, 370, 553, 683, etc.

121 *the outward signe of Bachus*: i.e. the long pole or ale-stake pro-
jecting above the door of a medieval tavern and surmounted by a 'bush',
a garland or bunch of evergreen. This was the *lure* which enticed
Hoccleve. The metaphor is borrowed from hawking where a lure (a
piece of leather decked with feathers to resemble a small bird) was
used to reclaim a falcon.

126 *daunger*: 'enforcement'. Cf. *OED* s.v. 1c and Chaucer's *General
Prologue* 663.

136 *chynchy*: 'niggardly'. The word first occurs in the Chaucerian
translation of *la Romant de la Rose* 479, 6002 etc., where it is properly
chiche, and cf. *chyncherie* in the *Regiment* 4743, Lydgate's *Bycorne
and Chichevache*, Trevisa's translation of *De regimine principum*
ii.18 (MS Digby 233, f. 29va), *auary and chynches*.

138 *Venus femel lusty children deere*: i.e. harlots. Cf. *Squire's Tale*
264.

143 *Poules Heed*: this tavern stood on the east side of Paul's Wharf
Hill, just south of the Cathedral and opposite Paul's bakehouse. In a
document of 1162 the *bracinum* 'brewhouse' of St. Paul's occupied
the site. Other references to *Poules hede* occur in 1444 (R.R. Sharpe,
Calendar of Wills in the Court of Husting, London, ii.503), in 1456
(*Historical MSS Commission, 9th Report*, 12, 27), and in 1598 (John
Stow, *Survey of London*, edited by C.L. Kingsford, ii. 12, 17).

146 *wafres*: i.e. spiced cakes. One contemporary recipe specifies cheese,
flour, white of egg, sugar, and ginger: see T. Austin, *Two Fifteenth-
Century Cookery Books*, EETS o.s. 91 (1888), p.39.

153 *Loues aart*: a common phrase, derived from Ovid's *Ars amatoria*.

160 A repetition of the *Nun's Priest's Tale* 394, but the saying was in common use and perhaps not original with Chaucer.

174-5 'because I was prevented by my cowardice which the weight of blows always depressed'.

181 'I did not find fault with my purchases'. Cf. the *General Prologue* 326.

190 *brigge*: not London Bridge, well over half a mile from the Paul's Head, but Paul's Wharf, 100 yards south of the tavern, described by Stow ii.13 as 'a large landing place, with a common stayre vpon the Riuer of Thames'. This sense of *brigge* is recorded from 1375.

209 *my yeeres be but yonge*: cf. the *Regiment* 1984; elsewhere, ibid. 946-7, he says, *Two partes of my lif and mochil I seur am, past ben.* Hoccleve wrote *La Male Regle* when he was about 35, and the *Regiment* six years later, and these poetic references to his 'youth' may be part of literary convention; a man's expectancy of life in the early fifteenth-century probably did not exceed 60 years. For the attitude adopted in the latter poem see p.115, below. Hoccleve died at 58.

225 *combreworldes*: 'those that trouble or encumber the world'. Cf. the *Regiment* 2091. The compound is possibly due to a misunderstanding of *Troilus* iv. 279, 'I combre world that may of nothyng serve', owing to the absence of the definite article before *world*. Cf. Lydgate's mis-understanding (in the *Epithalamium for Gloucester* 129 and *Fall of Princes* ii. 4861) of *daring don* in *Troilus* v. 837, copied by Spenser, *Shepherd's Calendar*, October 65 and December 43, *Faerie Queene* ii. 42 and vi. 37.

227 *sotil deceyuours*: among whom Hoccleve would certainly have placed Bushy, Baghot, Green, and others of Richard II's ill-fated council, and the rebels of 1403 and 1405. A more exotic example, which might have sprung to mind at this time, would have been the Old Man of the Mountain, whose story is retold in *Mandeville's Travels*, p.200.

233-4 *the Book of Nature of Beestes*: identified by Miss Hammond as Theobaldus, *Physiologus de naturis duodecim animalium*, where the allegorical interpretation of the Siren's *natura biformis* might have suggested to Hoccleve its relevance to his condemnation of flatterers.

245 *enuolupid in cryme*: cf. *Pardoner's Tale* 942.

249 *Holcote*: the story of Ulysses and the Sirens is related by Robert Holkot, *Super sapientiam Salomonis* 64. Hoccleve may first have heard of Holkot in a sermon; see G.R. Owst, *Literature and Pulpit in medieval England* (1933, reissued 1961); but he clearly owned or read a copy later. See note to 299. Chaucer also uses Holkot's commentary as a source in the *Nun's Priest's Tale* 451 ll.

269 'although they be somewhat too grievous'.

270 *priuee and appert*: 'in private and in public'. The phrase is a for-mula, as in the *Wife of Bath's Tale* 1114.

281 This general complaint, like the whole digression against flatterers, is probably part of the critical climate of the time, rather than a personal response to a private slight or even to recent political disturbances. See J. Peter, *Complaint and Satire in early English literature* (1953).

299 *This is my skile*: the progression through the sins that follows, and the rhetorical device of *gradatio* which it embraces, are borrowed from Holkot, *Super sapientiam Salomonis* 84.

301 *Malencolie*: the more common association is expressed by Chaucer's Parson, 'After glotonye thanne comth lecherie, for thise two synnes been so ny cosyns that ofte tyme they wol nat departe.' Cf. *Regiment* 3802–8.

308 *the Priuee Seel*: at times (and perhaps at this time) the *officium* of the Privy Seal, where the clerks worked when they were not at Westminster, and the *hospicium*, where they lodged, were in one building. Cf. 188, *hoom to the Priuee Seel*, and the *Regiment* 802, *In þe office of þe Priuee Seal I wone.*

321 *Prentys and Arondel*: younger contemporaries of Hoccleve, whose names recur in a petition to the Privy Council, dated 14 February 1431, and cited by Furnivall, p. xxxv.

349 *My thank is qweynt*: 'the gratitude of my guests is over'. One meaning of *thank* is specifically 'gratitude for entertainment or feast', cf. the second *Balade to Somer* 66.

352 *mene reule*: 'moderate regimen'.

354 *olde clerkes wyse*: cf. the *Tale of Melibee* 1214, 'For the proverbe seith, He that to muche embraceth, distreyneth litel.'

361 *Thy rentes annuel*: i.e. the annuity of £10. This is distinguished from the *lucre* of *manuel labour*, i.e. salary for a Privy Seal clerk, generally in arrear (cf. note to 420 below); its value was *vi. marc yeerly, mete and drinke and clooth* (*Regiment* 1217).

366 *yiftes*: the Privy Seal clerks occasionally received largesse from nobles and officials, generally for expediting their business, and shared in the confiscation of the goods of outlaws. One record of Hoccleve's share in such a confiscation, valued at £40, in 1398 is extant.

407 *sit*: a contracted form of *sitteth* 'befits'.

417 *my lord the Fourneval*: Thomas Nevil, lord Fournival, was appointed sub-treasurer on 13 December 1404, and was succeeded by Nicholas Bubwith on 16 April 1407.

421 *my yeerly ten pound*: Hoccleve was granted an annuity of £10 on 12 November 1399, which was replaced by one of 20 marks (£13.6.8) on 17 May 1409. It was generally paid in two instalments, at Easter and Michaelmas, and the records of its payment reflect the varying financial circumstances of the Exchequer, viz.

Michaelmas 1400 and Easter 1401, £8.15.3 on 13 December 1400.
Michaelmas 1401, £5 on 29 November 1401.
Easter 1402, £5 on 26 April 1402.
Michaelmas 1402, £4.18.9 on 7 December 1402.
Easter and Michaelmas 1403, £9 on 15 October 1403.
Easter 1404, £5 on 6 March 1404.

Because of a restriction on the payment of recent annuities enacted by Henry IV in 1405, the next recorded payment to Hoccleve is for Michaelmas 1405, £5 on 26 March 1406, closely followed by another for Easter 1406, £5 on 13 May 1406.

From these records, printed by Furnivall, pp.li–lxx, and from a Latin note in the margin of the manuscript, written by Hoccleve himself, *Annus ille fuit annus restrictionis annuitatum*, it is clear that the *Michel terme pat was last* was Michaelmas 1405. The poem was therefore written after this date, 29 September 1405, and before the receipt of the next payment on 26 March 1406.

423 *ferne yeer*: the historical background to Henry IV's restrictions on annuities is described by J.H. Wylie, *History of England under Henry IV* (1894), ii. 21–8.

Balade to Master John Carpenter

John Carpenter (1370–1441) was town clerk of London from 1417 to 1438 and a man of wide interests and many benefactions; see T. Brewer, *The Life and Times of John Carpenter* (1856). Among his books was a copy of *De regimine dominorum*, possibly a manuscript of Hoccleve's *Regiment of Princes*. J. Stow (*Survey of London*, i.327) reports that the pictures of the Dance Macabre with Lydgate's verses were painted about the cloisters of St. Paul's at his charge.

The balade is without any indication of date, but it clearly belongs to Hoccleve's free-spending bachelor days, possibly before the *bisy smert cotidian* that prompted *La Male Regle*. Its tone is decidedly friendly, like the *Balades to Sir Henry Somer*, and suggests an acquaintance formed in earlier days, perhaps at the Court de Bone Conpaignie.

Furnivall notes that in the first line '*Carpenter* is written over an erasure, the original having probably another name, to whose owner it had been sent, as it was doubtless afterwards sent to other moneyful folk.' This is certainly possible, but why Hoccleve should alter his own fair copy (if it is such) is not clear. Perhaps Carpenter's response was singularly generous.

2 *chalenges*: 'claims for payment'.

8 In the margin is written 'A de B et C de D, etc.', representing the names of Hoccleve's creditors which accompanied the original poem, probably with their debts itemized.

17 *aspen herte*: cf. the *Regiment* 1954 and note.

Balade to Sir Henry Somer (December 1408)

Henry Somer, a friend of Chaucer and formerly a clerk of the Exchequer, was appointed Keeper of the Privy Wardrobe on 13 February 1405 and a baron of the Exchequer on 8 November 1408. He was probably a friend of Hoccleve of many years' standing, and this friendly reminder of the overdue annuity was written, it seems, in December 1408. Hoccleve had been paid £5 on 7 July 1408, and was finding the customary delay of the next instalment as irksome as usual. Cf. *La Male Regle* 420, the *Balade to my Lord the Chancellor* 6, the *Regiment* 823, 4383. But, despite this spirited appeal to Somer, Hoccleve did not receive the Michaelmas instalment of his annuity until 13 February 1409.

The pun on 'Somer' and the balade and roundel built about it were possibly suggested by the roundel to summer at the end of the *Parlement of Foules*. If so, it was a happy inspiration which Hoccleve neatly and amusingly develops.

3 *nere*: i.e. the assimilated form of *ne were* 'were not'.

14 *Mighelmesse*: 29 September and harvest-time, when the 'harvest' of the clerks' annuities failed.

18 *suppoaille*: a variant of *suppowell* 'assistance, succour', recorded from 1375 to 1513, and frequently misunderstood by scribes and early printers.

21 *shippes*: a pun on the great noble, valued at one half-mark, issued by Edward III in 1344 to commemorate the naval victory off Sluys in 1340, and stamped with a large ship. The pun recurs in Lydgate, *Letter to Gloucester* 17, and, like the better known pun on angel, was probably in common usage.

22 *Port Salut*: 'Port Safety'. A humorous application of *portus salutis*, a phrase frequently applied to the Virgin Mary, cf. Chaucer's *ABC to the Virgin* 14 and Adam of Persenia, *Mariale* 127.

25-6 John Hethe served at the Privy Seal from 1387 to 1409 and at this time (1408) must have been a senior clerk. Thomas Baillay served there from 1392; this reference to him at the Privy Seal is the last known, cf. *Calendar of the Patent Rolls, Henry IV*, vol. ii, 1401–5 (1905), p. 50. For John Offorde see a note by J.H. Kern, 'Der schreiber Offorde', *Anglia* xi (1916), p. 374, and *Calendar of the Patent Rolls, Henry V*, vol. ii, *1416–22* (1911), p. 309; a letter possibly by him is printed by A.L. Brown, op. cit., p. 274.

Balade to Sir Henry Somer (April 1410)

This second balade to Somer, about to be appointed Chancellor of the Exchequer on 20 June 1410, is as friendly as the first. The contents of Somer's letter to the Court de Bone Conpaignie, of which Hoccleve and no doubt other government clerks were members, may be inferred from the first six stanzas: Somer regrets the recent lapse of the May Day feast which increasing expenditure and membership have imperilled, and suggests a revival of the custom on the coming May Day, a Thursday in 1410, pledging in his letter £2 for general expenses and promising in addition to pay his ordinary contribution. Possibly Somer wanted to revive the convivial custom, which he may have enjoyed as an ordinary member during his days as an Exchequer clerk, to celebrate his imminent promotion.

Hoccleve's reply, on behalf of the club, states that far from desiring any outrageous expense the Court is content to leave everything to the good judgement of Somer, who shall be the ruler of the feast.

This endearing glimpse into a minor medieval feast is hardly great poetry, but it does show how Hoccleve's verse can rise to an occasion, genial and urbane in tone, neat and competent in metre and rhyme. Undoubtedly the *balade* added to the pleasure of the feast. Regulations governing a comparable *court*, the Pui, are contained in the *Liber custumarum*, ed. H.T. Riley, *Monumenta Gildhallae Londoniensis* ii. 1. 216, Rolls Series (1860), and its possible relevance to Gower is discussed by J. Fisher, *John Gower* (1964), pp. 81–3.

6 *Vse*: another example of the plain infinitive. Cf. the note to *Complaint to the Virgin* 11.

8–14 'in the place of honour, the Temple, where excessive waste should not be permitted, first for refreshment and joy we were urged to spend freely; but we note you do not bid us be unreasonable.'

the Temple: possibly the Middle Temple, to which Chester's Inn belonged; see the *Regiment* 5.

Wheras nat. . . excesse: the Temple, then as now, was devoted to the law, and this legal joke would not be lost on Somer or others of the Court de Bone Conpaignie.

29 *six shippes*: i.e. six nobles of Edward III, otherwise £2. See note to the first *Balade to Somer* 21. This was a good and generous sum to spend on such a feast.

31 *flour or whete*: probably intended as a general term for food, including the meats.

47 *good*: 'substance, possession'.

66 *Reule*: 'give direction', the customary role of the master of a feast.

thank: 'gratitude expressed by your guests'. Cf. *La Male Regle* 349.

67 'order as much wine to be drawn as you wish'.

69 *tourn*: perhaps a play on the legal sense of *turn*, 'the twice yearly circuit' of a county sheriff. See *OED* sub *tourn*.

Three Roundels (perhaps 1408)

Chaucer's *Complaint to his Purse*, humorously modelled on the traditional lover's complaint to his lady, probably inspired the first two of these roundels, though there are similar *balades* by Machaut, Deschamps, and Froissart; see N. Wilkins, *One hundred Ballades, Rondeaux and Virelais from the late Middle Ages* (1969). Hoccleve achieves a lightness of touch by expressing his complaint as an exactly balanced question and reply within the briefest possible form of the roundel. Possibly he composed the piece as a catch-song for the entertainment of the Court de Bone Conpaignie or other habitués of the *Poules Heed*, and not as a suppliant poem to a patron.

The third roundel is more obviously satirical. The burlesque of this lover's praise of his lady is only fitfully applicable to *lady moneie*, and may have no connection with the other roundels; but see note to 31. While keeping the traditional catalogue form of description, for each generally admired female characteristic Hoccleve substitutes its opposite. His portrait of a loathly lady may be contrasted with that of the Prioress in the *General Prologue* 152–6, whose features are those of a beautiful heroine.

5 *of your prison the keye*: i.e. the clasp of my purse.

6 *streite*: 'strictly, securely'.

11 *saillen*: an oblique pun on the golden *shippes* mentioned in the *Balades to Somer* 21 and 29.

12 *ageyn this Cristemesse*: 'before this Christmas'. The phrase recurs in the first *Balade to Somer* 19, probably written in December 1408. It is not possible to identify the year, though it must have been between 1404 (the first Christmas that passed without payment of his Michaelmas annuity) and 1409 (when his annuity was increased). Perhaps this roundel was composed in 1408 in the same festive spirit as the first *Balade to Somer*.

13 *right a feynt gladnesse*: 'a very hollow humour'. *feynt*, variant of *feyned* from OF *feindre*.

19 *risshes three*: One of many contemporary expressions of utter worthlessness. Cf. *an hawe, a strawe, a bene, a leke*, and note to the *Regiment* 103.

20–21 'you held my great power in no respect while I was in your careless protection.'

24 *delauee*; 'dissolute'. Cf. *deslauee, Parson's Tale* 629. The word recurs in the *Regiment* 4624, the *Tale of Jereslaus* 901.

31 *my lady*: this lady seems to be *lady moneie*, and *hir golden forheed* seems to echo *my golden heed* in 28. Though not all of the lady's qualities are applicable to a gold coin, the general sense of abusive denigration would fit admirably with her previous rejection of Hoccleve's petition.

38 *pentice*: 'penthouse', which would shield her mouth from the rain even if she were lying on her back. It is just possible that the reference may include a private joke against his Privy Seal colleague Prentice. Cf. *Death and Life* 169.

44 *papeiay*: the screeching of the African parrot is attested in encyclopaedias and travel books of the time, and a few of these exotic birds had already been imported into England; Henry V's mother, Mary de Bohun (d. 1394), is known to have owned one. *papeiay* was also the name of the native green woodpecker, as in *Sir Thopas* 56, and this other sense may (though less plausibly) be intended here, cf. *papyngay* in Clanvowe's *Book of Cupid* 222 (ed. V.J. Scattergood, *The Works of Sir John Clanvowe* (1975), p. 85), in Lydgate's *The Churl and the Bird* 359 (ed. E.P. Hammond, *English Verse between Chaucer and Surrey*, p. 110 and note), and *Commendacion of Our Lady* 81. The inn of the abbot of Cirencester, on the north side of Fleet Street and just west of the Fleet, was known as the Popinjay in Hoccleve's time; the name survives today in Poppin's Court.

The Regiment of Princes (about April 1411)

It was originally intended to print in an appendix to these selections from the *Regiment* collated readings from all extant manuscripts, and these collations were made and their tentative conclusions printed in 1974

(*Transactions of the Edinburgh Bibliographical Society* iv. 263). The forthcoming critical edition of the *Regiment* now makes such an appendix superfluous. Accordingly, the textual apparatus here is limited to rejected manuscript readings and collated readings from MS Harley 4866 which generally exclude purely orthographic and inflectional variants. Where MS Arundel 38 lacks lines 4990–5118, the loss is supplied from MS Harley 4866; where the latter lacks lines 1–56, 2017–51, 2108–60, the collation is given from MS Douce 158.

MSS Arundel 38 and Harley 4866 are both carefully written verbatim (and at times almost literatim) copies of Hoccleve's lost holograph; they were written in or shortly after 1411, very probably under his general direction; they are seen to have, on reference to Hoccleve's extant holographs, a consistency of prosody, word-order, syntax, and closeness to his spelling system, which (apart from their early date) give them an unusual textual authority. All other extant copies of the *Regiment* are posthumous (i.e. made after 1426) and most of them were written after 1450. They all derive from the lost archetype independently of MSS Arundel 38 and Harley 4866, and their variant readings record successive stages in the scribal degeneration of the text. Their evidence is useful in determining which of two variant readings in the two early manuscripts is likely to be authorial, and which scribal; but in no case in the text of these selections does any of these posthumous copies offer a reading arguably superior to that of the base manuscript or its affiliate.

In the apparatus, which may be supplemented by reference to textual notes in the Commentary, these sigla are used: H = MS Harley 4866, D = MS Douce 158. The substantive emendations (at lines 14, 27, 1003, 1004, 1008, 2045, 2055, 2073, 2082, 4244, 4316, 4351, 4353, 4868, 4885, 4935, 4936) which are based on MS Harley 4866 are supported by readings from these representative manuscripts from other sub-groups: MSS Rosenbach, Digby 185, Douce 158, Additional 18632, Royal D 17. vi, Selden supra 53, with these variants: lines 14, 27, MS Selden supra 53 missing; line 1003, MSS Douce 158 and Selden supra 53 *ne hir*, MS Rosenbach *ne hym.* Line 4966, MSS Digby 185, Additional 18632, Royal 17 D.vi *tyme* resemble H *tymes.*

Throughout the poem, which must have taken some months to complete, Hoccleve refers to Henry as *my lord the prince*; his accession on 21 March 1413 thus gives one terminus for the date of composition. And a reference early in the poem (ll. 285–7) to *a wrecche not fern agoo, whiche pat of heresye conuyct and brent was vnto ashen drye*, who may certainly be identified as John Badby, burned at Smithfield on 1 March 1410, provides another terminus. Within these three years a more precise date can be determined from other references in the poem. Most important, Hoccleve complains sadly to the Old Man (ll. 821–5 and cf. 4383–5), while talking of his annuity of twenty marks, that *paiement is hard to gete adayes.* This annuity was granted on 17 May 1409, and payments of half-yearly instalments are recorded on 23 May and 22 November 1409, 17 July 1410, 8 July 1411; on 26

February 1412 he was paid the annual twenty marks at one time.
Earlier in his discourse with the Old Man (ll. 804-5, cf. 1023), he refers
to his twenty-four years' service at the Privy Seal *come Estren and that
is neer.* The only Eastertide within the years 1410-13 when he could
reasonably have complained about the uncertainty of his annuity was
1411, when Easter Day was 12 April; before Easter 1410 he was paid
regularly, and before Easter 1412 he had received his annuity in full,
while in 1413 Easter Day (3 April) must have occurred after the poem
was written, since Henry IV died two weeks previously on 20 March.
    Elsewhere in the poem (ll. 1881-2) Hoccleve refers to *th'ordenaunce,
longe after thys schal no graunt chargeable out passe.* Throughout the
summer of 1410, when money was scarce, the Council sat at London
under the direction of Prince Henry and examined, and put into effect,
plans for saving money by restricting annuities; see J.H. Wylie, *History
of England under Henry IV* (1894), iii.319-23, and K.B. McFarlane,
Lancastrian Kings and Lollard Knights (1972), pp. 78-101. A somewhat
similar restriction on annuities had been enacted in 1405; see *La Male
Regle*, notes to 420 and 423. In the context the reference to the
ordenaunce bears all the marks of a wound still fresh, and so confirms
the date of composition of the poem as 1411. A similar confirmation is
found in Hoccleve's advice to the Prince not to hold *your conseilles*
on the *holy dayes* (ll. 4964-5); the Prince ceased to preside over the
Privy Council 30 November 1411; see Wylie, iv. 88.

The Sleepless Night

The convention of the sleepless night as an introduction to a long poem,
generally within the allegorical structure of a dream, is subscribed to
by nearly all late medieval poets. But these sixteen stanzas which
describe the night before Hoccleve's meeting with the Old Man are far
from the conventional. Instead of a fictional lover uttering a traditional
complaint of distress, the poet in his own person (it seems) is expressing
a deep, almost Boethian lament on the fickleness of fortune and the dis-
tressful effects of *thouȝt* 'worry'. In particular, he is concerned about
his financial future, a preoccupation to which he returns frequently in
the poem, as in ll. 839-40:

> Now God helpe al. For but he me socoure,
> My futur yeeres lik ben to be soure.

These remarkable departures from the traditional nature of a medieval
poetic introduction are underlined by the exceptionally high quality of
the writing. The power of such lines as l. 80,

> Who so that þouȝty ys, ys wo begon,

where the intense reality of the poet's misery anticipates Keats by four
centuries, is related to the shell of its allegorical pattern by C.S. Lewis,
The Allegory of Love (1936), pp. 238-9.
    Yet the relation of this introduction to the whole poem must be
remembered. It creates the despairing context from which the Old Man

rouses Hoccleve by the force of Christian argument and directs him to write *a goodly tale or two* for Prince Henry. In both these directions Hoccleve is using the opportunity of verse to resolve a personal problem, much as Milton does in *Lycidas*. And also the introduction, by the very depth of its anguish, prepares for the traditional setting of the poem where the young man's problems are seen to yield to the old man's wisdom, in the familiar classical and medieval manner. Thus the departure from the traditional has a structural as well as a personal impetus. Not surprisingly, it is outstandingly successful.

4 *as I can vnderstonde*: a rhyming formula, normally used without personal reference.

5 *Chestres Yn*: according to Stow, ii. 92–3, 'neare adjoining to the sayd church (i.e. St. Ursula at the Strand) betwixt it and the riuer of Thames was an Inne of Chancery commonly called Chesters Inne because it belonged to the Bishop of Chester, by others named of the scituation *Strand Inne*. . . Than was the Bishoppe of *Chester* (commonly called of *Lichfield* and *Couentrie*) his Inne or London lodging.' Which of these two buildings is referred to by Hoccleve is hard to tell. Both stood on the site which is now Somerset House. Whichever it was, *Chestres Yn* seems to have been at this time both *officium* and *hospicium* of the Privy Seal; see note to *La Male Regle* 308. Hoccleve's subsequent references to *my pore cote* (the *Regiment* 845, 940), where presumably he removed on marriage, can scarcely be to the *hospicium*; the apparent contradiction would vanish if the *cote* were adjacent or close to the *hospicium*.

Stronde: from 1220 *le Stronde* is recorded as a proper name for the street, with houses and gardens adjoining the river, which ran between the cities of London and Westminster.

7 *Thog3t*: 'anxiety, worry'. This sense of the word is recorded from *c*.1220.

23 Richard II was deposed in Westminster Hall on 30 September 1399 before a great assembly (which may possibly have included Hoccleve, granted an annuity by Henry IV on 12 November 1399, perhaps as part of royal policy to commend itself to its servants); he was murdered at Pontefract in January 1400. His fall involved *many another lord* killed or executed as a result of anti-Lancastrian risings and plots.

26 *mene*: 'middling', cf. *pore*, l. 29.

27 'I could see none, but finally I saw'.

30 *storm of descendyng*: 'misery of being thrown (on Fortune's wheel) from prosperity'. A vivid phrase which intensifies the metaphor of the previous line, without in any way reconciling the poet to *pore estat*.

48 Cf. *Knight's Tale* 1533.

50 The phrase recurs in the *Letter of Cupid* 285 and, earlier, in *Troilus* ii. 659, *Sumnour's Tale* 2217, and *Pardoner's Tale* 510.

55–6 Cf. *Troilus* iii. 1625–8,

> For the fortunes sharp adversitee
> The worste kynde of infortune is this:
> A man to han ben in prosperitee,
> And it remembren whan it passed is.

58 *nusaunce*: 'annoyance, liability or power to harm'. The word recurs in the *Mother of God* 21 and the *Regiment* 2050, always in rhyme, and is first recorded in these passages.

63 *In o plyt*: 'in one state'.

67 *lawhyng*: 'smiling'. Cf. *Merchant's Tale* 1723.

75-6 'And so that I should not be alone against my will, Wakefulness offered his service.' This personification of *wach* is unrelated (it seems) to the idea of the Watch, i.e. the night guard of a medieval town.

82 *equypolent*: 'equivalent', which word is recorded from *c.*1425. The word, which recurs in the *Regiment* 5108, again in rhyme, is first recorded here, but cf. *equipolences* 'equivocation', *Romaunt of the Rose* 7076.

91 *To sorwe soule*: 'to grieve alone'.

103 *nat a pere*: cf. note to the *Three Roundels* 19. Elsewhere in the *Regiment* Hoccleve uses as expressions of proverbial worthlessness *flye* 613, *strawe* 622, 1670, *lek* 'leek' 1662, etc.

The Troubles of a Scrivener

Hoccleve tells the Old Man that if his annuity fails, he will be destitute; he knows nothing of farming, and moreover, the arduous labours of a scribe (which he now describes) have greatly affected his health. Since he remained at the Privy Seal until 1426 and the fair copies of his poems which belong to his later years (MSS HM 111 and 744 and Cosin V. iii.9) are beautifully penned, he is perhaps exaggerating his afflictions. On the other hand, he never appears to have enjoyed perfect health after his boozing days, and there are other witnesses of the scribe's unquiet life in the fifteenth century, like William Ebesham, William Worcester (alias Botoner), and George Ashby.

969-70 This implication of previous well-being, despite the erratic payment of his annuity and the penniless tenour of his verse, probably has some basis in fact. Cf. the *Regiment* 37. And after the increase of his annuity in May 1409 and his marriage and removal to a *pore cote*, he was probably free from the most pressing financial distresses. His problems were no doubt aggravated by his status. An educated man yet not a graduate, in close contact with the rich and the influential yet not gentle-born nor of independent means, the medieval government clerk must always have moved uneasily between the two classes of society.

974 *sixe marc yeerly*: the salary of the clerks was paid by the Keeper of the Privy Seal (at this time John Prophet, who succeeded Nicholas Bubwith on 4 October 1406) out of his own daily allowance of 20 shillings. There is no record of such payments to Hoccleve or his named colleagues in any of the Issue Rolls.

978 'scarcely could I scare away the hawk who would deprive me of my poultry.'

990 *Art*: 'skill, craft'.

The Old Man's Advice and Hoccleve's Address

The Old Man has told of his own troubled life and his patient acceptance of the will of God, in order to encourage Hoccleve's drooping spirits, and now offers some practical advice about ways of improving his drooping finances.

1867 *Chaucer* died on 25 October 1400, according to the inscription on his tomb in Westminster Abbey, where in a house in the garden he had lived since 4 December 1399, less than one mile from Chester's Inn.

1879 *py patent*: i.e. the annuity of 20 marks, granted 17 May 1409.

Hanaper: the department of Chancery which paid all the expenses of the Chancery organization. For details of its origin see T.F. Tout, *Chapters in the Administrative History of Medieval England* (1930), i. 286.

1881 *th'ordenaunce*: for the restrictions issued during the summer of 1410 see the headnote to this poem.

1900 *No maistry yt ys*: 'it is no great achievement or task', a common idiom, as in *Sir Beves* 1738, Lydgate's *Mirror of Our Lady* 17.

1912 This caution against flattery (which occurs in a context intentionally flattering to the Prince) recalls a similar passage in *La Male Regle* 210–288 and anticipates similar warnings in the fourteenth section of the *Regiment, De consilio habendo in omnibus factis*. In an age of gross flattery and sharp realism (the two things go together) Hoccleve seems to make a distinction, perhaps unconsciously, between the 'sincere flattery' a poor poet may offer to his patron and the 'evil flattery' of royal counsellors; but cf. *Julius Caesar* ii.1,

> But when I tell him he hates flatterers,
> He says he does, being then most flattered.

At the same time the caution is an obvious literary device by which a humble subject may justify his presumption in seeking to guide princely conduct, cf. Gower in *Vox Clamantis* vi, and Chaucer in the Prologue to the *Legend of Good Women* (F version, 373–413). The encouragement of tyranny by flattery is a concern of all who write *de regimine principum*, cf. John of Salisbury, *Polycraticus* iii. 15.

1914 *Salamon the wyse*: several different collections of proverbs ascribed to Solomon, in Latin, English, and French, were in circulation, but Hoccleve's side-note here specifically refers to Proverbs 29:5: 'Qui blandis fictisque sermonibus loquitur amico suo, expandit rethe gressibus suis.'

1921 A similar side-note refers to Proverbs 1:10: 'Fili mi, si te lactauerint peccatores, ne adquiescas eis.'

powke: the rhyme *sowke/powke* shows the word to be *puck* 'a wicked man' and not *poke* 'bag' in the sense of 'bag which hides a bad bargain'.

1924–5 Another side-note refers to Jeremiah 9:8: 'In ore suo pacem loquitur cum amico suo et occulte ponit ei insidias.'

1926 A side-note quotes Seneca, *De beneficiis* vii: 'Summa loca tenentibus maxime deest qui veritatem dicat. Adulacionis certamen omnibus officium est contencio vna omnium quis blandissime fallat.'

1933 Another quotation from Seneca, *ibid.* 'Ignorant seculi potentes vires suas, dum se credunt tam magnos quanti predicantur.'

1942-3 'You had better be far away than be guilty of this deception.' Jerusalem, as the most distant place of pilgrimage, apparently is used in much the same way as the modern Timbuktu, but the idiom is none the less unusual.

1954 Cf. the *Balade to Master John Carpenter* 17. Both cases are developed from the common simile, e.g. *Troilus* iii.1200, *Summoner's Tale* 3.

1957 *at his large*: 'at his will or liberty'. The idiom has earlier been used in the notable line 277, *walk at large oute of thi prisoun.*

1960 Cf. the *Regiment* 2078-9, W.W. Skeat in *The Athenaeum* 4 March 1893, p. 281.

1961-74 This eloquent lament is the first of three tributes Hoccleve pays to Chaucer in the *Regiment*, cf. lines 2077-107, 4978-98. It is also the first of many fifteenth-century tributes (the references to Chaucer by Scogan, *A Moral Balade* 67 and 97, being casual), all of which repeat the substance of Hoccleve's praise; see C.F.E. Spurgeon, *Five Hundred Years of Chaucer Criticism and Allusion* (1925), A. Brusendorff, *The Chaucer Tradition* (1925), and D.S. Brewer, *Chaucer and Chaucerians* (1966). There is no reason to doubt Hoccleve's claim to have been Chaucer's pupil; see p. 125, below. For an interesting speculation of Hoccleve's ownership of a manuscript of the *Canterbury Tales* see J.M. Manly and M. Rickert, *The Text of the Canterbury Tales* (1940) i. 168-9.

1964 *science*: 'knowledge'. The reference seems to comprehend both Chaucer's mastery of his techniques and the wide range of his reading, rather than to commend his writings on astrology, and echoes the praise given to Aristotle. Cf. 2087-90.

1968 The invocation to Death and the catalogue of his famous victims (here limited to one) are literary variations on the classical *ubi sunt* theme, adopted from the French, and become common in later English medieval poets.

1975 *my mayster Gower*: Gower died before 15 October 1408. The phrase may indicate a personal acquaintance. For the last 11 years of his life Gower lived with his wife within the Priory of St. Mary Overies (now St. Saviour's), Southwark, where he is buried, and Hoccleve was one of the scribes of the T.C.C. manuscript of the *Confessio Amantis*: see Doyle and Parkes, 'The production of copies...'. In two obvious ways Hoccleve's *Regiment* reflects Gower's *Confessio Amantis.* The Old Man and the Confessor have a common function within their poems, and Gower's Book Seven is based on the pseudo-Aristotle, *Secreta Secretorum.* But in all essential respects the two works have little in common. Gower's serious and mature octosyllabic couplets and his unvarying concern with classical example make Hoccleve's pleasant, idiomatic, gossiping rhyme royal stanzas seem youthful and vigorous by comparison.

The absence of the names of other London poets who died before 1411 suggests that there were none of note during Hoccleve's residence, although a number of minor poets, like Sir John Clanvowe (d. 1390), Henry Scogan, Sir John Montague, were certainly writing at the time. And the subsequent overwhelming rise to fame of Lydgate seems to have cast a long shadow over the literary renown of the capital which did not recover its former glory until the Tudor usurpation. Cf. Dunbar's *Lament for the Makaris*.

1983 *fourmeel*: 'acquainted with the rules of art'. Cf. Gower, *Confessio Amantis* iii. 89.

1990 *hye tyme*: i.e. nearly 7 in the evening. The discourse has lasted most of the April day.

2007 *at the Carmes messe*: 'eat at the Carmelite refectory'. The Carmelites or White Friars occupied a large site just east of the Temple, extending from Fleet Street to the river Thames. Hence *heere* indicates that Hoccleve and the Old Man had returned from walking in the fields and were each a few yards from their *mete*.

2015 *hote*: 'fresh'. Cf. the *General Prologue* 687.

2027 *thrystyth*: 'desires vehemently', cf. 2047. The meaning survives in the biblical phrase 'hunger and thirst after righteousness'. The absence here, and in the Wyclif translation of Matthew 5:6, of the new idiomatic proposition *after* is historical; the OE construction of verb with genitive lost its inflexion in ME.

2031–3 Cf. a similar remark by the Old Man 1994–5.

2034–7 Hoccleve's regret that he has no money nor costly gift to recommend him to the Prince refers to the commonly accepted practice of the time, that a suitor or suppliant should recompense as richly as possible the energies and favours to be expended on his behalf.

2039 *Hys episteles*: i.e. the pseudo-Aristotle, *Secreta Secretorum* (also known as *De regimine principum*, cf. *hys book of gouernaunce* 2051 and the title of Hoccleve's own version). The revival of Aristotelian teaching in thirteenth-century Europe and the increasing interest in the nature of kingship combined to produce the *Secreta Secretorum*, based on the Alexander legend (conveniently summarized by Vincent of Beauvais in Book Four of his *Speculum Historiale c.* 1250) and dating in its extant Latin form from the fourteenth century. Both Latin and French translations circulated in late medieval England, where the unstable political climate gave the book an immense appeal. It was translated into English many times; by Gower, *Confessio Amantis*, Book 7, in 1390; anonymously *c.* 1400 and again *c.* 1460 and by James Yonge *c.* 1420, which three translations are edited by R. Steele, *Secreta Secretorum*, EETS e.s. lxxiv (1898); by Gilbert Haye in 1456; by Lydgate and Burgh *c.* 1450; by John Shirley *c.* 1440; and in two other anonymous versions, extant at Oxford (MSS Ashmole 396 and University College 85, part 2); see M.A. Manzalaoui, *Secretum Secretorum: Nine English Versions*, EETS o.s. 276 (1977).

2040 *gold in cofre*: a metrical tag, cf. the *General Prologue* 298, *Man of Law's Tale* 26, *Legend of Good Women* 380.

2042-4 The syntax would read more easily if the inversion *To sette was* were emended to *Was to sette*, but the word order and rhythm of the MS seem to be Hoccleve's.

2052 *Gyles, of regiment of princes*: like the *Secreta Secretorum*, the *De regimine principum* of Aegidius de Columna (d. 1316) was extremely popular in the Middle Ages. It had already been translated into English by John Trevisa (d. 1402), whose version is studied in an unpublished thesis by H.E. Childs, 'A Study of the Unique Middle English Translation of the *De Regimine Principum of Aegidius Romanus*' (University of Washington, 1932). Trevisa's work was known in London, where his *Gospel of Nicodemus* was incorporated by John Shirley into one of his manuscripts, and Hoccleve may have had the Trevisa text beside him, much as John Walton (Trevisa's successor at Berkeley and translator of Vegetius, *De re militari*) used Chaucer's translation of Boethius in 1410 to produce his rhymed version. Hoccleve's poem is a summary of the ideas of Aegidius de Columna, intermingled with his other sources and his own personal reminiscences and illustrations. See F. Aster, *Das Verhältniss des altenglischen Gedichtes 'De Regimine Principum' von Thomas Hoccleve . . .* (Leipzig, 1888).

2053 *plotmel*: 'a piece at a time, piece by piece'. The word is only recorded here. Cf. *piecemeal*.

2058 *chyldhode*: 'ignorance, inexperience'. Cf. *La Male Regle* 64.

2060 *pamfilet*: used again to describe the *Regiment* by Hoccleve in the *Balade to Edward duke of York* 1.

2082 *irriparable*: the word is first recorded here. Significantly, it is in rhyme. Cf. *equypolent* 82, *nusaunce* 58. The second *i* in the scribal form may be an error, cf. the more common *irreparable* in other manuscripts of the *Regiment* and OF *irréparable*.

2085 *rethorik*: i.e. the skilful use of language in which the 'colours of rhetoric' (various combinations of word and phrase, derived from the stylistic practices of classical writers and used to point the meaning and embellish the expression of medieval books) are authoritatively handled. The pre-eminent example of successful rhetorical writing in English is Chaucer's *Troilus*. The subject was one of the seven liberal arts studied in medieval universities and formed, with grammar and logic, the basic *trivium* of the syllabus. In addition, it was explained and expounded in numerous handbooks, of which the Englishman Geoffrey de Vinsauf's *Poetria Nova* c. 1225 is perhaps the most famous.

   Tullius: i.e. Cicero, whose practical expression of stylistic splendour was the more admired in the Middle Ages as the perfect illustration of the rhetorical theory expounded in his *De inventione* and in another handbook, *Rhetorica ad Herennium*, falsely attributed to him.

2088 *Aristotle*: the rediscovery of the works of Aristotle and his Arabic commentators revolutionized the study of theology and philosophy in thirteenth-century Europe, and in these fields Aristotle became the undisputed master. Cf. Chaucer's Clerk of Oxford, the *General Prologue* 295, and note to 1964 above.

2089 *Virgile*: Virgil's literary reputation, undimmed in the Middle Ages, was inflated even farther by numerous legends attracted to his name. See D. Comparetti, *Vergil in the Middle Ages* (translated by E.F.M. Benecke, revised edition, Florence 1946).

2091 *combreworld*: 'troubler of the world'. See note to *La Male Regle* 225.

2097-8 'than to a vicious renowned profligate, the worst that might be found'. On this sense of *tried* 'pre-eminent, distinguished' cf. *Sir Gawaine and the Green Knight* 4.

John of Canace

This tale, longer than all others but otherwise typical of the illustrative anecdotes inset in the *Regiment*, occurs in the eleventh section, *De virtute largitatis et de vicio prodigalitatis*. The basic ideas of this section are traditional enough, but implicitly in the suggestion to reward those who spend their lives in the king's service (4173-4) and explicitly in the confession of his own foolish generosity in times past (4355-65) Hoccleve gives them a personal interpretation.

The source of the anecdote is *De ludo scaccorum* iii. 8, translated by Caxton as the *Game and Playe of the Chesse* in 1474; and in one form or another (the most famous being that of Lear and his daughters) it was very common in the Middle Ages. In retelling it Hoccleve has moulded it to his own style. A straightforward tale without digression, its spirited movement is matched by its fluency of dialogue, and in detail and general effect it is crystal-clear. In its unpretentious way it is an ideal *exemplum* of *fool largesse*, since it plays first on the foolish generosity of the father and then on the hypocritical generosity of the children; and the way in which this doubling overflows the *moralitas* and allows John of Canace to outwit his avaricious daughters is entirely medieval.

4182 *Canace*: unidentified. Boccaccio, *De montibus*, sites a fabulous Mt. Canatus in Spain. And as a lady's name Canace occurs in Gower, the *Squire's Tale*, and elsewhere.

4197 'so that he did not limit his expenditure.'

4202 *disshed*: i.e. *dis-shed* 'dispersed', cf. *wasted* in some MSS, which supports the sense. The word is not recorded elsewhere in this sense, and its vigorous metaphor is possibly original.

4217 *daungere*: 'enforcement'. Cf. *La Male Regle* 126.

4223 Cf. *Troilus* iii. 616.

4262 *on hys nayle*: perhaps 'from his thumb-nail', to see if the coins rang true when spun from the thumb to the floor.

4282, 4285, 4287 *hym*: MS *hem*. Hoccleve distinguishes between the singular pronoun *hym* and the plural form *hem*. But such distinction was not universal, especially in East Anglia where the scribe of this manuscript (MS Arundel 38) seems to have come from. The forms are emended here and elsewhere for clarity, but they are not (*pace* A. Brusendorff, *The Chaucer Tradition* (1925), p.14) scribal errors.

4299–300 'Now it was decided that they should share the expenses of a joint household, the father excepted.' Cf. 4313–16. *helde house*, cf. modE 'keep house'.

4322 'And at once, before my body is carried hence.'

4324 *Prechours*: i.e. Dominican or Black friars.

4325 *þe Freeres Greye*: i.e. Franciscan friars.

4326 *Carmes*: i.e. Carmelite or White friars. Why they should receive only fifty pounds, is not clear. These 'legacies' were not, of course, provided by John of Canace but by his heirs themselves, and give a final, posthumous twist to the old man's deception, as well as ensuring his proper burial and the saying of masses for his soul. The neat duality of this ending is characteristic of the more polished medieval story-teller, and was present in Hoccleve's source.

4337 *so moot I the*: 'so may I prosper'. A common ME formula.

4340 Cf. *Sir Perceval* 2095.

4347 *pekked mood*: 'became angry'. See *OED* sub *mood* 2b.

4349 *sargeantes mace*: i.e. the staff of office of a minor town officer (not to be confused with a sergeant-at-law), made of wood and possibly covered with leather. The sumptuous silver mace of modern ceremonial gives a totally false comparison; John of Canace's mace was valueless.

De consilio habendo in omnibus factis

This fourteenth section of Hoccleve's poem is printed in its entirety and corresponds, in very general terms, to the ideas expressed by Aegidius de Columna, *De regimine principum*, book III, part 2, chapters 16–19, which Trevisa (MS Digby 233 ff. 144^V–147) translates exactly.

4885 *the ryches sawe*: 'the advice of the rich man'. Cf. 4893 *the poores sentence* 'the wisdom of the poor man'.

4890 *thys*: 'this man'. A gallicism, cf. OF *cis*.

4907 *yt ys no lesse*: 'it is no lie'. A metrical formula.

4920 *bryge*: a variant form of *brike*, cf. ONF *brique*, 'trap, gin, snare', and *brygelees* in the *Remonstrance against Oldcastle* 164.

4930 This curious simile is supported by a side-note, which Hoccleve seems to have misunderstood: 'scriptum est quod consilium bene potest freno compari', where the sense is of a bridle restraining impetuosity or imprudence.

4942 *holy wryt*: i.e. Proverbs 12:5, quoted in the margin.

4947 This warning against young counsel (which echoes complaints made against Richard II's favourites) contradicts the sense of 4881. But the medieval mind would have seen no logical objection to the general proposition that youthful counsel is bad, though good counsel should not be spurned merely on account of a youthful advocate.

4948 The side-note quotes 1 Kings 12:10, concerning the iniquities of King Jeroboam I of Israel.

4956 *the werre*: 'the worse'. It was accepted, even admired practice to rhyme identical forms of different words, i.e. *rime riche*.

4979 *in caas sembable*: cf. *Confessio Amantis* i. 6. E. F. Jacob, *Henry V and the Invasion of France* (1947), p.32 sees here a reference to the

Prince's great conciliar activities during the summer of 1410 (see head-note to the poem, p. 115, above). This is very possible, since Aegidius makes no reference to councils held on holy days.

4987 *ful many a lyne*: i.e. Chaucer's *ABC to the Virgin*, the Invocation to the Virgin which begins the *Second Nun's Tale*, and the prayer to the Virgin which begins the *Prioress's Tale*.

4990–5019 These lines were accompanied by a marginal three-quarter-length tinted drawing of Chaucer, framed within a panel. The whole leaf has been excised. The text is here printed from MS Harley 4866, with spellings altered to conform to the spelling conventions of MS Arundel 38.

4995 *hys lyknesse*: this likeness of Chaucer in MS Harley 4866 was made in or shortly after 1411 at London or Westminster under Hoccleve's supervision for presentation to a royal patron. In its details it resembles the famous equestrian portrait of Chaucer in the Ellesmere manuscript (Huntington Library MS EL 26.6.12).

The Harley likeness has a panel-type border and a checkered green background, which forms an imaginative contrast to the drab-coloured gown (perhaps now faded). Chaucer's right hand, pointing at Hoccleve's mention of the *resemblance* in the text, breaks the border of the panel in a deliberately casual manner found elsewhere in early fifteenth-century illuminated manuscripts in England. The details of this likeness (the position of the body and hands, the cap and gown, the penner and pendant, the forked beard) closely resemble those of the Ellesmere likeness, and the differences are minor; in the Harley likeness Chaucer's left hand holds a rosary, whereas in the other his right hand holds the reins, and the puckish charm and yellow hair of the Ellesmere head have been replaced by a more sober, even Socratic white-haired appearance. A relationship between these likenesses is not in doubt, and it is probable that they are the work of one artist. As the style of illumination in MS Arundel 38 is imitated from that of the Ellesmere manuscript, all three manuscripts (MSS Arundel 38, Harley 4866, EL 26.6.12) were probably illuminated in one atelier in London or Westminster.

Both the Harley and the Ellesmere likenesses are possibly independent copies, by one artist, of a panel portrait painted in Chaucer's last years. The authenticity of detail (of stature, beard, gown, pendant) is likely to be generally sound; they are partly supported by Chaucer's own references to his person in his poetry and vouched for by Hoccleve's accompanying lines. However, no great reliance can be placed on the artist's expression of the face in these posthumous copies, however great the temptation to discover the actual man. The portrait is discussed more fully in a forthcoming study, *Portraiture in fifteenth-century English illuminated manuscripts*.

4999–5003 This orthodox explanation of the *ymages pat in þe chirche been* defends one of the practices under attack by the Lollards at this time. See 5006–9 and the *Remonstrance against Oldcastle* 409–24. 'Mandeville', p.227, makes a similar defence against Saracen objections, which were the ultimate origin of Lollard compaints.

5019 *God sende vs pees*: in July 1411 John the Fearless, duke of Burgundy, sought English help in the French civil wars, and a small English force of 2,800 men was dispatched in October. See E.F. Jacob, *The Fifteenth Century 1399-1485* (1961), pp. 111-12, and the *Remonstrance against Oldcastle*, note to 9-10.

Two Balades to King Henry V (1411 and 1416)

The first *balade*, printed from MS HM 111 and occurring in almost all manuscripts of the *Regiment* which do not lack the relevant leaf, is properly an *envoi*. Hoccleve undoubtedly had in mind the *envoi* of the *Troilus*, itself the latest example in a long literary tradition which stretched from Boccaccio to Ovid. Hoccleve preserves the convention of poetic humility which seeks to deprecate envy.

The intricate rhyme-scheme (*ababbcbc*, veering to *cbcbbaba*, etc. to give catch-rhymes between stanzas) employs only three rhymes. This is the traditional pattern of the *virelai*, and Hoccleve's virtuosity in this rare type of English verse is further demonstrated in *balades* to Sir Henry Somer and Henry V (pp.25-8, 53-4, 58-60) and in a *balade* to 'my lord the chanceller' (not printed here). Other *balades*, though lacking the catch-rhymes that distinguish the *virelai*, show similarly intricate patterns of limited rhymes, e.g. those to Henry V and Edward, duke of York p.71, 67). The latter reproduces the scheme of Chaucer's *Anelida and Arcite*, ll. 220-55, 281-316, and cf. the *envoi* to the *Clerk's Tale*.

The only other recorded English *virelais* are the 'Lover's Lament' (beg. *Alone walkyng, In thought pleynyng*) and a *balade* attributed to Richard, earl of Warwick. The *virelais* mentioned in Chaucer's *retraccioun* are lost, though both the cited sequences of stanzas in *Anelida and Arcite* are immediately followed by *virelai* patterns, viz. ll. 256-71, 317-32, and it may not be entirely fanciful to see Chaucer's example reflected in these *balades* of his pupil.

This rhyming virtuosity and the sudden flow of poems on state occasions between 1413 and 1415 suggest that Hoccleve had achieved a recognized position as a court poet, which his illness then eroded. Certainly, his confessions of 'simplicity', in this one particular at least are demonstrably conventional, and in a wider reference his fondness for catch-rhymes parallels his syntactical linking of stanzas, both indicating a sense of sophistication which the comparative simplicity of diction and theme does much to hide.

The second *balade*, printed from MS HM 111 and also found in MS Fairfax 16, was written sometime after Henry's return from Agincourt on 23 November 1415, and probably before Hoccleve's illness late in 1416. The *bille* was certainly a petition for payment for official expenditure on parchment, ink, and wax. Such reimbursements were paid to Hoccleve during Henry V's reign on 17 January 1414 (for £1.6s.8d.), on 14 February 1417 (for £2.6s.8d), on 10 July 1419 (for 12s.), and on 23 February 1422 (for £2.0s.11½d).

8 *vs three*: perhaps Prentys and Arundel, mentioned in *La Male Regle* 321. A list of Hoccleve's contemporaries at the Privy Seal is given by A.L. Brown, p.262.
Newgate: one of the London prisons for debtors.

Balade to Edward, Duke of York (1411)

The identification of *my gracious lord of York* and *worthy prince Edward* with Edward, duke of York, killed at Agincourt at the age of 42, is certain. The only other Edward to hold the dukedom of York during Hoccleve's lifetime was born in 1411. This *balade* is an *envoi* added to a presentation copy of the *Regiment* and, like the *envoi* to John, duke of Bedford, which it closely resembles in detail, it uses the formal nine-line stanza.

1 *litil pamfilet*: cf. *Regiment* 2060. Medieval English books varied from unbound quires like the *Libel of English Policy* to huge compilations like Trevisa's translations of Higden's *Polychronicon* and Bartholomæus Anglicus, *De Proprietatibus Rerum*. By the side of these latter volumes the *Regiment* would appear small, though doubtless Hoccleve does not intend the disparaging reference to indicate more than a conventional poetic humility.

11-14 The occasion, of which nothing more is known, recalls Gower's meeting with Richard II on the Thames and the subsequent command to write the *Confessio Amantis*. By giving the duke a whole book instead of a few *balades*, Hoccleve doubtless hoped to deserve a larger reward, and the duke's death at Agincourt may have been another of those misfortunes which blighted the poet's hopes of preferment.

17 'be a spokesman for my concern'. *owtere*, which recurs in the *Dialogue* 175, is 'utterer', cf. *OED* s.v. *outer* sb[2].

23 *my gracious lady*: i.e. Philippe (d. 1431), second daughter and co-heir of John, second lord Mohun. She married Walter, fourth lord FitzWalter (d. 26 September 1386), Sir John Golafre (d. 18 November 1396), and Edward, duke of York (d. 25 October 1415), and was clearly a personable and wealthy lady. But no other literary tribute to her is known, nor is she known to have owned manuscripts, though Edward of York certainly did.

32 'I am not, even with you, much closer to my purpose.' cf. *Regiment* 2119, *My witte therein is but litille the nere*, and *OED* sub *near* adj.

33-5 'And if you will not be my messenger, then I shall omit my respects, and I certainly would not wish that. Prince Edward, not I, shall determine whether you see my lady or not.'

40 *my maistir Picard*: like *my maistir Massy* in the next *balade*, presumably the member of the ducal household to whom Hoccleve submitted his manuscript, and possibly an intimate secretary with some literary pretensions. *Pekeard* is the name of the scribe of BL MS Harley 2386, part 1 (a collection of Latin historical notes written during the reign of Henry V), but to identify *my maistir Picard* with this man would be speculative. Other references to *Pycard* and *Pykard* are noted in F.J.

Furnivall, *Hoccleve's Works, The Minor Poems* (1892, revised 1970), p. l., and by C. Peterson, 'Hoccleve . . . and the *Pearl*-poet', *RES* n.s. xxvii (1977) 49-55. This Thomas Pycard, perhaps the same as John Pycard clerk, is mentioned in the Old Hall manuscript (MS. Additional 57950) as an early fifteenth-century composer of mass music used by the royal household, and is author *c.* 1424 of a rhymed acronym for Alice (born *c.* 1404), daughter of Thomas Chaucer (MS. Additional 16165 f.248).

46-51 These disparagements are repeated in almost identical terms in the *envoi* added to the *Regiment* presented to John, duke of Bedford.

51 *colours*: i.e. the colours of rhetoric, for the skilful use of which Hoccleve admired Chaucer. See note to the *Regiment* 2085. Apart from metaphor and apostrophe and similar figures of speech which more reflect the living language than the rhetorical manual, Hoccleve rarely attempts the more sophisticated 'colours'. One exception is the *gradatio* employed in *La Male Regle* 299 where it is directly copied from Holkot; see note. Some discussion of Hoccleve's use of 'colours' is given by Mr. J. Mitchell, *Thomas Hoccleve*, pp.60-2.

55 *foul book*: this reference with the subsequent confession about his vain refusal to wear spectacles (the *Dialogue* 249) suggests that Hoccleve wrote the manuscript presented to Prince Edward himself. No holograph of the *Regiment* is extant, and within the conventions of the time a precise meaning to the *foul book* cannot be pressed. Possibly this description and explanation, here as in the *envoi* sent to John, duke of Bedford, is wholly rhetorical.

69 *thousand*: a polite and humorous exaggeration.

Balade to John, Duke of Bedford (1411)

Written in the same metre, for the same purpose, at the same time, and with the same expression of ideas (weakened sight, appeal to *my maistir Massy*, apologies for the absence of rhetoric) as the previous *balade*, this *envoi* was placed at the end of the copy of the *Regiment* presented to John, duke of Bedford (d.1435). This manuscript is not certainly extant; it may be MS Harley 4866 (an almost exact reproduction of MS Arundel 38) which lacks the first leaf, on which the recipient's coat-of-arms probably appeared, and the last leaf, which may have contained the *envoi*.

8 *custumed bysynesse*: i.e. the daily work in the Privy Seal office. BL MS Additional 24062 is a collection of official documents, mainly in French, which passed under the Privy Seal during the reigns of Richard II, Henry IV, and Henry V, and which are there copied *secundum composicionem Thome Hoclyf. facta per manum suam*. It is edited by Miss E.J.Y. Bentley (Emory Ph.D., 1965): *Dissertation Abstracts* 26 (October 1965) 2154b-5a.

10 *my maistir Massy*: otherwise unknown. Cf. the previous *envoi* 40. See T. Turville-Petre, 'Hoccleve, Maistir Massy . . .', *RES* n.s. xxvii (1975) 129-33, and C. Peterson, loc. cit. There seems no good reason

to identify him with that Thomas Massy of Roxton, Lancs., a clerk of Oxford, who held the living of Warrington in 1437; see A.D. Emden, *A Biographical Dictionary of Members of the University of Oxford from A.D. 1176 to 1500* (1957-9).

More Balades to King Henry V (1413 and 1414)

The first *balade* celebrates the homage accorded by the English peers to Henry V on his accession, 21 March 1413. Hoccleve probably wrote the poem beforehand. The imperative tone of the piece continues the exhortation of the *Regiment* which the central stanzas seem to summarize.

17 *sheeld and wal*: derived from OE *sceldweall* 'a formation of ranked shields guarding a chieftain'. Cf *Troilus* iii. 479–80.

25 *your modir*: i.e. Holy Church, as an interlinear *scilicet ecclesiam sanctam* says.

The occasion of the second *balade* is not certain. The Order of St. George, the most exclusive of medieval chivalric orders, assembled in the presence of the king when he was in England and of his regent when oversea. Henry V was in England from his accession, 21 March 1413, to 7 August 1415, from 16 November 1415 to 1 August 1417, from 1 February 1421 to 10 June 1421.

During these years the most important meeting of the Order was at Windsor on 24 May 1416, when the emperor Sigismund, in England trying to reconcile Henry V and the French, was installed as a Knight of the Garter, but at that time Hoccleve's illness had probably begun (see p.134, note to 40). Moreover, the absence of the epithet 'victorious' from the descriptions of the king and the underlying concern with the Lollards suggest a date earlier in the reign, possibly just after Oldcastle's attempted *coup d'état* on 10 January 1414. Lines 19–22 favour the latter interpretation.

In its metrical arrangement, where the rhymes of the four stanzas are identical (*-esse, -our, -alle*), Hoccleve perhaps imitates Chaucer's *Balade to Rosamounde*, though such identical rhyme-schemes are common.

3 Justinian (d. 565) founded and over-generously supported Christian institutions and zealously persecuted heretic and heathen, and so ensured the unwavering approval of the late Middle Ages. The reference is amplified in the *Remonstrance* 185-92; see note to 25-32, below.

10 Constantine I (d. 337), the first Christian emperor, was particularly esteemed in English folklore as the son of St. Helena, supposedly a British lady, responsible for the Invention of the True Cross.

17-18 Henry's reputation as an orthodox suppressor of Lollardry began while he was still Prince of Wales, when he supervised the burning of John Badby at Smithfield on 1 March 1410; see p. 114, above. And after his accession his energetic measures against the Lollards inspired the taunt 'prince of priests:; see p. 132, note to 289. For a modern comment on both these reputations and on Henry V generally see K.B. McFarlane, *Lancastrian Kings and Lollard Knights* (1972). pp.102-33.

25-32 The action taken against the Lollards before and during the Leicester Parliament in April 1414 did not, despite Hoccleve's plea, include a specific prohibition of the discussion of religious matters. But the episcopal power to arrest and suppress unlicensed preachers and books and to check heresy in whatever guise it should appear was already unlimited, and proved sufficient to contain (if not utterly to destroy) the Lollard threat. The stanza underscores the earlier reference to Justinian whose edict against disputation, in terms similar to those proposed here, is incorporated into the argument of the *Remonstrance* 185-92. See W.W. Skeat, *The Complete Works of Geoffrey Chaucer* (1897), vol. vii *Chaucerian and other Pieces*, pp. xl-xli, 501-2.

The Remonstrance Against Oldcastle (August 1415)

The poem, printed from MS HM 111, is edited separately by L.T. Smith, 'Ballad by Thomas Occleve to Sir John Oldcastle A.D. 1415', *Anglia* v (1882) 9-42. The rubric dates the poem; Henry V went to Southampton in July 1415 and embarked for France on 7 August; but a later reference in line 500 suggests that the poem (or at least the second part) was written after Henry's arrival in Normandy, in the Seine estuary near Harfleur, on 13 August.

Oldcastle, formerly a distinguished soldier and friend of Henry V before becoming a Lollard leader, was arrested in September 1413 for heresy but escaped from the Tower on 19 October. A Lollard plot, in which he was probably involved, to surprise the king at Eltham on 9 January 1414, was easily foiled, but Oldcastle remained at large until November 1417. He was executed on 14 December 1417. An excellent account of the Lollards and Oldcastle is given by K.B. McFarlane, *John Wycliffe and the Beginnings of English Non-conformity* (1952), pp.160-85.

Hoccleve's poem states the orthodox case against Lollard heresies, and may be compared with similar documents printed by A.W. Pollard, *Fifteenth-Century Prose and Verse* (1903). It may have been written with official prompting; though the conspiracy of Cambridge and Gray had been quashed, Henry could not have relished the possibility of a Lollard rising in England while he was in France, and it would clearly have been politic to regain Oldcastle's allegiance. Hoccleve does not attempt conversion solely by exhortation and denigration; but his reasoning against Lollard opinions and his appeals to Oldcastle to return to his old allegiance (from which wicked-doers have seduced him, a detail which seems to confirm the earlier hints of a personal pardon; see note to 261) had no practical effect, except as propaganda against the Lollard cause. In this latter context V.H.H. Green, *Bishop Reginald Pecock. A Study in Ecclesiastical History and Thought* (1945), pp.103-4, considers the poem 'the most telling of the replies . . . to Lollard preachers'.

The poem may be compared, in general terms, with Lydgate's *A Defence of Holy Church* (147 ll.), probably composed after the Lollard disturbances of 1413 and 1414; for which see J. Norton-Smith, *John Lydgate Poems* (1966), pp.30–4 and 150–4. Lydgate's poem is shorter, more literary, less personal; Hoccleve's poem speaks directly to the purpose with passionate conviction. The differences are characteristic. It is possible that in writing the *Remonstrance* Hoccleve is seeking to surpass Lydgate.

9–10 After distinguished service on the Welsh border, Oldcastle was one of the English captains sent by Henry Prince of Wales to help the duke of Burgundy's successful expedition against Paris in October 1411. See E.F. Jacob, *The Fifteenth Century 1399–1485* (1961), p.111.

33 In the margin Hoccleve quotes St. Augustine, *De fide ad Petrum*: 'Firmissime tene et nullatenus dubites, quemlibet hereticum et cetera qui ecclesie catholice non tenet vnitatem, neque baptismus neque elemosina quantumcumque copiosa neque mors pro Christi nomine suscepta proficere poterit ad salutem.'

48 *Conquere*: 'regain'. Cf. 498.

51 *Theodosius*: a marginal note cites Aurelius Cassiodorus, *Historia Tripartita* ix.30.3: ed. R. Hanslik, *Corpus script. eccl. lat.* 71 (1952) 541.

84 *Holy writ*: Hoccleve quotes Luke 17:14, 'ostendite vos sacerdotibus'. But, as 'Mandeville' notes of the followers of Jacob Baradæus, a sixth-century Syrian Monophysite, a different opinion might be held from Psalms 32:5, 111:1, 118:28. The Lollards may have been influenced by *Mandeville's Travels*, which began to circulate in England c. 1375, though the encouragement of heresy was not one of the author's aims.

95–6 *in the wal of heuene . . . Thou shalt a qwik stoon be*: in a side-note Hoccleve gives the source of the metaphor, St. Augustine, *De visitatione infirmatorum*, which in English translation seems to have circulated widely c.1400. See C. Horstmann, *Yorkshire Writers* (1896) ii.449–53, to whose list of manuscripts may be added C.U.L. MS Dd. 1.17, part 2, f. 31rb.

103–4 The metaphors are from wrestling, the popular sport in which Chaucer's Miller excelled (the *General Prologue* 548).

129 *I putte cas*: 'I postulate the circumstance'. The usage survived until Dickens at least, as in *Great Expectations*. The hypothesis anticipates a fuller discussion (ll. 321–44) of a genuine Lollard grievance.

143–4 The advocacy of heresy by humble artisans, weavers, shoemakers, and the like, was particularly resented, and merely by associating with such people Oldcastle magnified his sin in official eyes. Among those associated with Lollard activities in Bristol, Northampton, and London were several scriveners, limners, and parchment-makers (trades specifically concerned with the production of books), and it is possible that Hoccleve was personally and professionally acquainted with some of them. Thomas Marleburgh, for whom he wrote twenty-one lines *de beata virgine*, was a London stationer and master of the guild of Limners and Textwriters in 1423.

186 A side-note quotes 'Nemo', properly the *Institutiones* of Justinian: 'Nemo clericus vel militaris vel cuiuslibet alterius condicionis de fide christiana publice turbis coadunatis et audientibus tractare conetur in posterum ex hoc tumultus et perfidie occasionem requirens et cetera, et ibi expressatur pena in huiusmodi causis exequendis.' Cf. the *Balade to Henry V* on the order of St. George, notes to lines 3 and 25–32, above.

195–8 A similar list of books, owned by Sir John Fastolf in 1450, is printed by H.S. Bennett, *The Pastons and their England* (1932), p.111.

Lancelot de Lake: the thirteenth-century OF prose *Lancelot* was the source of most Lancelot romances, including the three fifteenth-century English ones, *Lancelot of the Laik*, *Le Morte Arthur*, and Malory's *Book of Sir Launcelot*.

Vegece: i.e. Vegetius, *De re militari*. See the Dialogue, note to 561.

The Seege of Troie or Thebes: Benoît de Sainte-Maure, *Roman de Troie* and Guido delle Colonne, *Historia destructionis Troiæ* (1287) were the medieval sources of all later accounts of Troy, including Lydgate's *Troy Book* (1420). And Statius, *Thebaid* and the OF *Roman de Thebes* were sources for tales of Thebes, such as Boccaccio's *Teseida*, Chaucer's *Knight's Tale*, and Lydgate's *Siege of Thebes* (1422). Hoccleve may refer to the contemporary English prose translations, but it is worth noting that he was bequeathed a manuscript of *De bello Troie* in 1392.

203–5 These six chronicles of the Vulgate Old Testament contain tales of valour and piety which, Hoccleve believes, will turn Oldcastle from doctrinal matters to more knightly pursuits.

212 *soules norice*: cf. the *Squire's Tale* 347.

228 A side-note quotes a supporting dictum of Constantine, possibly taken from an unidentified chronicle: 'Deus vos constituit sacerdotes, et potestatem dedit vobis iudicandi, et ideo nos a vobis iudicamur. Vos autem non potestis ab hominibus iudicari.'

240 *the princes two*: i.e. Constantine (l. 217) and Henry V (l. 234–5).

257 After the abortive rising of 9 January 1414 a list of traitors, headed by Oldcastle, was proclaimed on 28 March, and on 14 June he was formally outlawed at Brentford. The reference is to the Lollards who were taken and executed at that time.

261 The promise of pardon if Oldcastle would surrender to the King's mercy was proclaimed on 9 December 1414 and again on 18 February 1415.

273 The stanza begins with a large capital initial marking a new section or point of emphasis in the poem. Hitherto Hoccleve has emphasized the unreasonableness of Oldcastle's position and the unlimited mercy available to a repentant, and written more in sorrow than in anger. Now, in more vigorous mood, he refutes and condemns the Lollard beliefs. This second part may have been added later; see headnote on p.129.

289 *Prynce of preestes*: the phrase was not certainly used by Oldcastle, though it was entirely in character. Its use by the Lollards in reference to Henry V reflects his extreme orthodoxy.

337 *shoo the goos*: 'shoe the goose', a proverbial phrase for ridiculous interference.

369-76 There is no evidence of *flesshly lustes* among the Lollards, apart from Oldcastle's confession before Archbishop Arundel of his youthful lechery (Pollard, op. cit., p.182), and the charge seems to belong to that familiar pattern of denigration by which governments undermine the standing of their opponents. Hoccleve was possibly naïve enough to believe the charge.

384 *of dirknesse the lanternes*: an illuminating paradox. Cf. *ydil bysynesse* 451, though *ydil* may there mean 'wicked'.

387 i.e. the plot of 9 January 1414, which produced an abortive rising in St. Giles' Fields.

393-5 On these Lollard objections see J. Crompton, 'Lollard doctrine, with special reference to image-worship and pilgrimages' (Oxford B. Litt., 1950); W.R. Jones, 'Lollards and images', *Journal of the History of Ideas* xxxiv (1973) 27-50; A. Hudson, *Selections from English Wycliffite Writings* (1978), pp.179-81.

417-21 Hoccleve's own sight was defective (*Balade to duke of York* 55-63, *Regiment* 1029), but he was too vain to wear spectacles, known from 1352.

465-6 Rumours of a Lollard uprising after the discovery of the plot of Cambridge and Gray in July 1415 had no foundation. But their planned participation in that plot, and in particular Oldcastle's role as a leader of troops (thwarted by the Worcestershire levies summoned to Hanley Castle by the lord Abergavenny, whose descendant George, d.1535, owned a manuscript of Hoccleve's *Regiment*), were enough to justify men's suspicions.

498 'regain merit and honour'. Cf. 48.

504 *rial viage*: 'royal expedition'.

The Complaint of Hoccleve (November 1421)

This first poem of the 'sequence' is printed in its entirety from MS Selden supra 53 fos. 76-83ᵛ. This manuscript is carefully corrected by erasure and interlinear additions, and is punctuated by solidus at the half line and point at the end of the line. Its texts of the 'sequence' are very close, apart from minor spelling differences, to those of Hoccleve's holograph, MS Cosin V.iii.9, which lacks its original first quire containing the *Complaint* and part of the *Dialogue*; these missing verses were restored by the antiquarian John Stow (d.1605) verbatim but not literatim from MS Selden supra 53 or a very close affiliate.

The *Complaint* is also found in these manuscripts, listed with the sigla used in this edition:

B MS Bodley 221 fos. 1-6ᵛ (possibly copied from L)

C Coventry City Record Office MS fos. 40ʳᵇ-43ᵛᵃ

L MS Laud Misc. 735 fos. 1–5 (lacks ll. 74–146)
Y Yale University MS 493 fos. 1–6^V
Fragments of the poem are reported by Miss Hammond, op. cit., p.57 to be in MS Phillipps 8267. The *Complaint* is edited from MS Cosin V.iii.9 by Miss M.R. Pryor, 'Thomas Hoccleve's Series: an edition of MS. V.iii 9', unpublished dissertation (UCLA, 1968), and in part (ll. 1–308), in modernized spelling and with useful notes, by J.A. Burrow, *English Verse 1300–1500* (1977), pp.266–80.

The date of composition is determined by the reference in line 55 to the poet's recovery of his wits *at all halwe messe was fiue ȝeere*, i.e. 1 November five years ago, and to the *ende of Nouembre* in line 17; by the record of the Pells Issue Roll for 18 July 1416 that Hoccleve's annuity was then paid to him indirectly through friends; and by the date of the sequent *Dialoge* in March or April 1422.

The 'complaint' or *planctus* is a specific, even technical term in medieval poetry, denoting a formal, rhetorical expression of grief where the rhetoric is employed to assuage as well as to define. Hoccleve's *Complaint*, which has been partly shaped by Isidore's *Synonyma* (see note to l.310), relates a genuine personal experience. P.B.R. Doob, *Nebuchadnezzar's Children: Conventions of madness in Middle English literature* (1974), pp.208–31, comments on some conventional aspects of Hoccleve's description of his illness and suggests that his account is fictional. This conclusion is untenable. It ignores the roll of 18 July 1416 which authorizes an extraordinary loan to Hoccleve as well as an extraordinary method of payment of his annuity at a time when he says in the *Complaint* he was ill; the veracity of all other personal statements by Hoccleve in his verse; the credibility essential for the sequence of poems intended for Duke Humphrey which such a fiction would destroy; the development in late medieval England of the concept of the poetic *persona*, sustained by Hoccleve's verse on all other occasions, in which such a fiction would be wholly anarchronistic; and the imaginative context of Hoccleve's other verse in which such a fiction is inconceivable.

The nature of Hoccleve's *wilde infirmite* is unknown. He mentions only the one symptom of amnesia: *the substaunce of my memorie wente to pleie as for a certein space* (ll. 50–1). It lasted for several months, beginning after 29 February 1416 and before 18 July 1416, and ending with complete recovery on 1 November 1416. It may be that in early 1416, having completed a major work and several minor poems on state occasions and still without preferment, he was under particular strain from exhaustion and disappointment, and that in such a context his affliction was more of a mental and nervous collapse than a certifiable illness. One of the causes of madness in the Middle Ages was thought to be *of to grete studie and of drede*, reported by Bartholomaeus Anglicus vii.6 *de amencia*, as translated by John Trevisa, *On the Properties of Things* (1975) i. 350, cf. iv. 11 *de melancholia*, ibid. i. 161–2.

Whatever its nature, the illness is merely the starting point of the *Complaint* which is substantially and movingly concerned with the suspicions of his friends of his recovery and his grief at those suspicions. It does, however, make a sad and ironic counterpoint to the gay apostrophe to *Helthe* which is one of the themes of *La Male Regle*, and certainly confirmed Hoccleve in his conviction of *this worldes chaunge and mutabilitie* (l. 117) and his already apparent tendency towards melancholia.

The opening stanzas may be compared with the beginning of the *Regiment*. In both poems the season and weather serve to heighten the mood of *the þouȝtful maladie* and introduce a 'debate' which resolves, within the poem, a personal problem. The sincerity of the poet's grief and the modesty of his manner are here forcefully conveyed in some of the most powerful lines in fifteenth-century literature.

1-7 This stanza forms a sharp, intended contrast to the opening lines of Chaucer's *General Prologue*.

40 *the wilde infirmite*: i.e. the mental illness which overtook Hoccleve some time after 29 February 1416 and before 18 July 1416.

44 *counseil*: 'secret'.

47 *pilgrimages*: apart from the famous shrines at Canterbury and Walsingham, numerous English shrines of less importance were supposedly endowed with healing powers by the presence of holy bones and other relics, and promises of pilgrimage to them and other shrines hallowed to various saints, especially those dedicated to the Virgin Mary, were generally made in times of sickness and distress.

72 *Westmynstir Halle*: where cases before the courts of Common Pleas, the King's Bench, and Chancery were heard, and where in a corner the clerks of the Privy Seal sometimes worked.

78 *þe sauter*: a side-note quotes Psalm 30:12: 'Qui videbant me foras fugerunt a me. Obliuioni datus sum sicut mortuus a corde. Factus sum tanquam vas perditum quoniam audiui vituperacionem multorum commorancium in circuitu.'

88 *suche age*: i.e. about 47 when he recovered his wits. Hoccleve had another five years to live when he wrote this poem.

91 *hem vnwar*: the construction, historically an OE dative usage, resembles the Latin ablative absolute. Cf. 375 and *La Male Regle* 67.

99-101 'God alone who knows the secrets of every heart knows what shall befall, whatever men think or imagine.'

123 *bukkissh*: OE *bucca* 'male goat, deer' gives an adjective *buckish* 'lecherous', recorded from 1515. But the sense of this earlier occurrence is rather 'wild, given to sudden starts', cf. *wilde steere* 120, and *MED* s.v. 'haughty, overbearing', and *EDD* s.v. 'hobgoblin, bogey'.

124-6 'and it is fitting to put him among (*lit.* in the row of) those who give an opinion without reason.'

143 *a leke*: cf. the *Regiment* 1662 and note to 103.

152 *Thouȝ*: 'as if'.

154 Cf. the *Complaint of the Virgin* 221.

163-8, 170-5. The use of soliloquy to present opposing arguments, cf. ll. 185-9 and 191-3, is first found in the *Troilus* ii.703-63 and 771-805, as Professor Burrow notes.

197-8 'I may not prevent a man's imagination leaping over the moon, if he wishes.'

217 *commvnynge*: 'talking'.

242 *peere*: a play on 'peer' and 'pear', although the secondary sense forces the rhyme. See note to the *Regiment* 103.

257 *blowe*: 'blown'. The metaphor ultimately refers to the trumpet of Rumour.

310 *a book I sy*: identified by A.G. Rigg, 'Hoccleve's *Complaint* and Isidore of Seville', *Speculum* 45 (1970) 564-74 as the *Synonyma* or *Soliloquia* of Isidore of Seville, edited in *Patrologia Latina* lxxxiii. 825-68, where the man complains (like Hoccleve, ll.197-210) of the general willingness to accept false rumour without proof, and (like Hoccleve, ll.176-82) of the need to keep silent in face of provocation.

318 *encomborus*: cf. the *Regiment* 466. OF *encombros* 'distressing', borrowed by Chaucer in *House of Fame* 862 and the *Complaint of Venus* 42, and imitated by Lydgate as well as Hoccleve.

337 *al this fare*: 'all this stuff'. An idiom in common use.

375 *Me of his hast vnwar*: cf. 91 and *La Male Regle* 67.

The Dialogue with a Friend (March — April 1422)

The extracts from this poem of 826 lines are printed from Durham University Library MS Cosin V.iii.9, written by Hoccleve himself and sent to Joan, countess of Westmoreland. The presentation copy which he undoubtedly gave to Humphrey, duke of Gloucester, does not survive, but other manuscripts of the complete 'sequence' of poems (of which this Dialogue is the second) are extant; pp.132-3, above. Miss Hammond prints lines 498-826 of this poem from MS Selden supra 53, with useful notes.

The poem may be dated by a reference in line 136 to a newly passed act of Parliament against coin-clipping (which was signed in November 1421) and by Hoccleve's confession of his age as 53 in line 246. A further reference to Gloucester's return from France is seen, in the light of these earlier references, to indicate this second return after 27 March 1422: see note to 662.

A Tribute to Humphrey, Duke of Gloucester

This tribute to the patron to whom the whole sequence of poems was addressed reflects the martial glory which Gloucester won in Normandy. As a soldier, a lover of books, and an admirer of women, Gloucester shone with the splendour of an Italian renaissance prince during Henry V's reign; his later ensnarement and checkmating by the Beaufort faction during and after Henry VI's minority and his subsequent death in 1447 (probably by poison) form one of the minor tragedies of medieval England, notwithstanding the partisan praise of Tudor historians. See K.H. Vickers, *Humphrey Duke of Gloucester* (1907) and H.S. Bennett, *Six Medieval Men and Women* (1955).

533 Gloucester's initial appointment as *custos Anglie* on 30 December 1419, to replace John, duke of Bedford, whose advice was needed at the framing of the Treaty of Troyes, lapsed with the return to England of Henry V on 1 February 1421. In June 1421 he accompanied Henry to France, whence he returned after 27 March and before 23 April 1422, once more to replace as *custos Anglie* his brother John, duke of Bedford, who again went to advise the king in France. In the autumn of 1422 he married Jacqueline of Hainault. Hoccleve is referring to his second return and appointment as *custos Anglie*, *pace* Doyle and Parkes, op. cit., p.182, note 39; against lines 543–4 Hoccleve adds in the margin *scilicet de secundo redditu suo de ffrancia*.

556 This reference to Gloucester's generosity to Hoccleve is an early testimony to his reputation as a patron of letters and a lover of books; see R. Weiss, *Humanism in England during the Fifteenth Century* (3rd edn., 1966), pp.39–70, and R. Hunt and A. de la Mare, *Duke Humphrey and English Humanism in the fifteenth century* (1970). Hoccleve very probably presented him with a copy of the *Regiment* in 1411. Until Henry V's accession in 1413, as the fourth and youngest of the royal sons Gloucester took little part in public affairs.

558 *As sad as any stoon*: 'as unmoving as any stone'. A variant of the more common metrical formula (translated from the troubadours' phrase) *still as stone*. Gloucester's abandonment of Jacqueline of Hainault in 1428 (when the pope pronounced the marriage invalid) for Eleanor Cobham destroyed much of his popularity in London. Hoccleve, like Lydgate in his contemporary *Epithalamium for Gloucester* (for which see E.P. Hammond, op. cit., esp. pp.142–5), is writing at the height of the duke's popularity.

561 *Vegece*: i.e. Vegetius, *De re militari*, a fourth-century compilation of ancient military sources, which enjoyed a great vogue in the Middle Ages, especially as a manual of siege warfare. It was translated into French by Jean de Meun and by another, and into English by John Walton in 1408 (MS Douce 291; another copy written for the Pastons by William Ebesham before 1469 is extant in MS Lansdowne 285) and printed by Caxton in 1489; a version in rhyme royal was made c. 1460 (R. Dyboski and M.Z. Arend, *Knyghthode and Bataile*, EETS o.s. 201 (1935), and a Northern English translation c. 1500. Hoccleve probably knew of, and possibly refers to, Walton's translation. In the *Remonstrance against Oldcastle* 196 he had advised the heretic to read the work.

563 When Gloucester landed in France in 1415 with Henry V, he was 24 and without military experience. But at Harfleur, Agincourt, Cherbourg, and Rouen his personal bravery and his direction of siege artillery were so distinguished that he was regarded as one of the outstanding soldiers of his day.

567 *Chirburgh*: Cherbourg surrendered to Gloucester on 1 October 1418 after a lengthy siege. Its capture concluded the victorious expedition under Gloucester sent by Henry V to subdue the Cotentin in March 1418. Gloucester had marched north from Vire, through Torigny, St. Lô, Carentan, and Valognes, with the Earl of Huntingdon in support on his left flank.

573-4 'This prince is by deed as well as by blood the true descendant (follower) of duke Henry, so worthy and good.' *Duc Henri* is Henry, the first Plantagenet Duke of Lancaster (d.1361), a father-in-law of John of Gaunt, cf. *Regiment* 2647-53.

576 *Constantyn*: i.e. the Cotentin peninsula. See note to 567. The intrusive *n* in the first syllable is due to analogy with *Constantynople*, also called *Costantynople* (e.g. by 'Mandeville').

592 The date of Gloucester's birth is not recorded. His father Henry Bolingbroke received the news on 1 November 1390 at Königsberg, having left England the previous July to fight against the heathen Lithuanians, and a birthdate in August or September thus seems probable. But at what times during these months the planet Mars was in the ascendant is (so far) undetermined, and in any case this information would still be too imprecise to discover the exact date; see W.C. Curry, *Chaucer and the Medieval Sciences* (2nd. edn., 1960), pp.172-85. Medieval confidence in the belief that human direction was determined at one's nativity by the stars in their courses must have been greatly heartened by Gloucester's influence by *bataillous Mars*, both in his successful campaigning and in his less happy marriages and his probable murder. Astronomical tables relating to Gloucester survive in MS Sloane 407, fos. 224-7.

596 *Humfrey*: for this somewhat forced play on the words *homme ferai* compare *Mara* in the *Complaint of the Virgin* 183. Both are typical examples of the fashionable medieval habit of name-questing.

610 *the seege of Roon*: after the surrender of Cherbourg, Gloucester joined Henry V before Rouen, where he was given command of the Porte St. Hilaire sector on the north-east of the town. His tent was pitched nearer the walls than the neighbouring royal headquarters, and in the contemporary accounts of the siege (by Titus Livius, the humanist in the duke's service, who wrote a life of Henry V; by the pseudo-Elmham, another royal biographer; and by John Page, whose eye-witness account is written in verse, printed in *Archaeologia* xxi (1827) 48-78, xxii (1828) 361-84) special mention is made of Gloucester's personal bravery. Hoccleve had probably read John Page's poem as well as listened to the gossip of returning soldiers. Rouen surrendered on 20 January 1419. Thereafter, the fighting increasingly gave place to negotiations leading to the Treaty of Troyes, sealed on 21 May 1420, and as soon as the preliminary alliance with Phillip, duke of Burgundy, was signed on 25 December 1419, Gloucester returned to England as *custos Anglie*: see note to 533, above.

620 *ascance*: here used (cf. *asaunces* 'as if' in *Troilus* i.205 and 292) as an intensive adverb, cf. *indeed, in no way*, the word is of un-

uncertain origin and meaning, see *OED* sub *askance*. Miss Hammond, op. cit., p.407, suggests that it may be an exclamatory imperative like *Begone*! Hoccleve may have used the word thus, perhaps equating it with *a chance*, and cf. *do way*.

The Friend's Advice

662 *lente*: in 1422 Ash Wednesday was 4 March and Easter Day 12 April, and within these dates the poem was composed. The more general ME meaning of 'spring' is possible, but clearly the context favours the religious sense, with its suggestion of repentance.

667 *wyt*: 'blame'. Cf. OE *wite* 'punishment, pain, blame'. As Hoccleve explains later in the poem (ll. 750–84), any objection that in the *Letter of Cupid* he who merely translates the words of Christine de Pisan dispraises women, can only be held in defiance of the text. But the accusation makes a convenient literary situation, probably copied from Chaucer's studied repentance in the *Legend of Good Women* and devised to pay a pleasant compliment to Gloucester (ll. 703–7) while forging a link with the rest of the 'sequence'. To pretend to have decried the sex and then to apologize was a polite poetic fiction, which developed in part from the anti-feminism of Christian apologists and goliardic poets; and according to the French tradition (which Hoccleve follows in the *Letter of Cupid*) Englishmen were arch-offenders. Such a *motif* was, of course, attractive to the educated women who seem to have formed the larger part of the medieval audience for romances and polite literature. Apart from some bawdy punning of his own in the *Letter of Cupid*, the comic exaggeration in the Roundels, and the invectives against Fellicula in the *Tale of Jonathas*, Hoccleve maintains a sympathetic attitude towards women in his verse, as in the *Regiment* 5104-194, cf. the ironic ambiguities of Chaucer.

669 *quarter sak*: i.e. a sack capable of holding a quarter (8 bushels) of grain.

691 *To make partie*: 'to take sides against, match'. A gallicism, cf. *faire partie*.

693 'they have humbled better men than you.'

696 *vice*: the reference is to the *Wife of Bath's Prologue* 662, 'I hate hym that my vices telleth me', and not (as Miss Hammond, p.407, states) to the *Tale* 955, where *vyce* 'defect' has an entirely different meaning.

703-7 This playful compliment to Gloucester clearly precedes his wooing and marriage of Jacqueline of Hainault in the autumn of 1422. At that time he was 32, a late age for a medieval nobleman to contract a first marriage, and there were doubtless good personal reasons for his delay; at 25, exhausted by his early indulgences, he had followed a dietary prescribed by his physician Kymer, printed in *Liber niger scaccarii*, pp.552-9. Nothing is known of his irregular liaisons, except that with Eleanor Cobham, his mistress from 1425 and his wife from 1428. Hoccleve, of course, is merely hinting at the duke's social gallantries, undertaken within courtly circles *in honestee*. If he knew things of his patron that conflicted with the sharply expressed views on lechery in the *Regiment*, he prudently ignores them. See note to 558, above.

707 As a lover of books and patron of the arts and scholarship Gloucester was the outstanding figure of his age; see Vickers, op. cit., 340-425, Bennett, op. cit., Emden, op. cit. ii.983-4. And the habit of lending and discussing books seems to have been common in courtly circles; on the fly-leaves of a FitzAlan copy of the *Regiment* (MS Royal 17 D.vi) are inscribed the signatures of various borrowers of the book in the fifteenth century, and cf. Hoccleve's *Complaint* 372-5. Gloucester, as Protector during the minority of Henry VI, was probably responsible for the granting of the corrody to Hoccleve in 1424, and was the first of eight members of the Council who signed the enabling warrant.

The Tale of Jonathas (perhaps before 1422)

This poem of 672 lines, the fifth and final poem of the 'sequence', is printed from MS Cosin V.iii.9, omitting ll. 1-84 (Hoccleve's introductory stanzas) and ll. 456-672 (the story of Jonathas' revenge). It occurs in the five other manuscripts of the complete 'sequence' (see p.132) and, with the *Regiment* and the *Tale of Jereslaus*, in MSS Royal 17 D.vi and Digby 185. It also occurs with the *Tale of Jereslaus* in MS Eng. poet. d.4, which lacks lines 111-75, 187-201, 214-62.

The poem contains no internal evidence of dating, and may have been written before Hoccleve evolved the idea of the 'sequence'. The story is taken from the *Gesta Romanorum*, compiled in England *c.* 1300, of which version MS Harley 2270 is perhaps the best text. Three manuscripts of a fifteenth-century English prose version exist; see S.J.H. Herrtage, *Gesta Romanorum*, EETS e.s. xxxiii (1879), where this tale is printed on pp.180-96. Hoccleve's prose *moralitee* which follows his poem corresponds very closely to the independent *moralitee* of the prose version.

Hoccleve follows his source (cf. MS Harley 2270 fos. 46^v-49^r, tale 54) closely. Where Chaucer perhaps would have summarized the bequest and the prince's departure in a vivid opening paragraph and shown more diversity and development of character and motive, Hoccleve is content to let the story for the most part make its own way forward under the weight of its fairly obvious allegory. Some alterations he does make, as in the details of the wooing, and possibly greater change (for example, the young man's emergence from doting love to a finely matured revenge) would have imperilled the allegory, explained in the *moralitee* at the end. As it stands, Hoccleve's version is brisk and interesting, especially when compared with other stories from the *Gesta Romanorum* told by Gower and Lydgate, and is not an unworthy successor to Chaucer's tales in rhyme royal. Mr. J. Mitchell, op. cit., pp.91-5 comments on Hoccleve's use of his source here.

85 *an emperour*: named Godfridus in the Latin and English prose versions.

92 Death-bed scenes of princes are a dramatic and didactic common-place in medieval romance.

101 Magic rings, brooches, and carpets and similar artefacts feature predominantly in eastern tales, the ultimate source of much of the *Gesta Romanorum*, and in the more exotic European romances. Cf. the *Squire's Tale*.

144 'but wise wommen do not grieve deeply'. This reference may be intended literally. But cf. 300–3. The details of the mother's grief are added by Hoccleve.

155 *the studie general*: i.e. the *studium generale*, a centre of study where students from all parts gathered to follow the *trivium* (grammar, rhetoric, logic) and the *quadrivium* (arithmetic, geometry, astronomy, music). See H. Rashdall, *The Universities of Europe in the late Middle Ages* (revised by A. B. Emden, 1936) i.6.

159 *a morsel of plesance*: cf. the *Regiment* 3434 and Dunbar's possibly derivative 'morsall of delyte'. The phrase is a spirited equivalent of *quedam mulier pulchra*, cf. the prose version 'a faire woman'. A similar translation occurs in the *Letter of Cupid* 237 where Hoccleve writes 'the foulest slutte in al a town', cf. *femmes foles, de peu d'honeur, males, maurenommees*.

The basic metaphor has many modern parallels (e.g. bit, tart, crum-pet), listed by E. Partridge, *A Dictionary of Slang and Unconventional English* (5th. edn., 1961). But in these encounters medieval under-graduates were not always the dupes, cf. the sad case of Margery of Hereford, cited by J.E.T. Roger, *Oxford City Documents 1268–1665* (1891), p.154.

162 *had a tale*: 'struck up a conversation'. The modE phrase 'to tell her a tale', used in similar contexts, possibly derives from this usage, cf. 167.

164 *pykid . . . to the sale*: 'dressed for market'. See OED s.v. *picked* ppl. a. 2 'adorned, exquisitely apparelled'. The metaphor is probably agricultural in origin.

168 The line is a conventional disclaimer. Cf. *Romant de la Rose* 5898, the *Knight's Tale* 2810. But for all his modesty Hoccleve contrives to paint a striking portrait of a medieval amorous encounter, none of which is found in the *Gesta Romanorum*.

177 *Fellicula*: a diminutive (or corruption) of *Felicia*. In the allegory she is carnal joys, and Jonathas a Christian man. His ring, brooch, and cloth represent faith, the Holy Ghost, and perfect charity. Hoccleve's form, for which he gives a false etymology 634–7, probably represents the scribal form in his manuscript of the *Gesta Romanorum* which may yet, if still extant, be thus discovered. In other manuscripts she is merely *amasia* 'lover, mistress'.

185 The time-honoured reference to *virginitee* is in the source, but the implication that a more experienced youth would have questioned its truth and relevance, cf. 225–7, is Hoccleve's addition.

192–3 A standard observation of the times, generally supported by a host of biblical precedents.

risshe: 'rush'. Cf. the *Three Roundels*, note to 19.

251 The reference to God, cf. 343, is found in the source, where it foreshadows the allegorical explanation at the end.

432–41 This *exclamatio* and dependent *consolatio* are added by Hoccleve.

433 *maad hath thy berd*: 'has deceived thee'. The idiom was common, cf. prologue to the *Wife of Bath's Tale* 361.

SELECT GLOSSARY

Obsolete words and words not easily recognizable from their scribal forms are recorded here. Forms which differ from the cited forms only by the addition of final *-e* are not listed. Past participle forms with the prefix *i-* and *y-* are recorded separately after those letters. þ follows *th*, ʒ follows *y*.

abiect, rejected, spurned
abit, abides
abregge, abridge
abreggynge, abridgement
acate, purchases, bill
adaies, by day
adoun, down, on the ground
adrad, afraid
aduocatrice, aduokett, intercessor
aduoutrie, adultery
affesid, afraid
affright, frightened
aftirclap, consequence
afyn, compose, refine
agast, agastid, frightened
ageyn, again, before, in preparation for, in anticipation of
aght, aught
agilt, betrayed
ago, agoon, passed
agrysed, terrified
akith, aches
algate, at least, always
alight, came down, alighted
allegen, allegge, allay
almesse, alms
anguysch, anguish
annoyeth, annoys, harms; annoyen, harm
anoyes, grievous disadvantages
aourned, adorned
apaid, apayd, satisfied
apalle, appall, appallist, make pale
apere, appeire, appear
apparteneth, belongs
appert, evident, open
areest, stay, stop
arettist, impute
argh, fearful
arghnesse, fear, awe
armonye, harmony

arte, cause; artid, caused; artith, causes
ascance, *see note, Dialogue* 620
aspen, ashen, of the ash-tree
assay, trial, proof, doubt
assoill, answer, satisfy, absolve
asterte, escape
as tid, immediately
astreit, at once
aswage, lessen
aswithe, as swythe, quickly
attame, tame, subdue
attempree, temperate
attemprely, moderately
atyr, attire, clothing
auctour, auctrice, author(ess), authority
auante, boast
audience, hearing
auys, advice, counsel
auyse thee, take heed
auysid, advised, informed
aventure, at risk, in trial
awayt, ambush
axe, ask; axeden, axid, asked; axit, axith, asks; axynge, asking

bagge, bag, purse
bapteeme, baptism
barwe, barrow
bataillous, warlike
bayte, rest, solace
beden, bade
beede, bid
beer, bore
begon, beset; wo begon, affected by woe
behight, behiʒt, promised
be-iapyd, tricked
bere, bear
bet, bettre, better

cacche, ensnare; **cacchynge,** snaring
calates, drabs, old women
canstow, canst thou
careful, full of care, anxious
carkeis, carcase, body
cas, caas, fortune, plight; **putte cas,** hypothesize
caste, intended
caytif, wretch; wretched
cessid, ceased
chalanges, demands
charge, cost, expense, business, burden
charge, lay a blame or duty upon
charre, scare
cheer, good fellowship, cheer, bearing
cheerly, with love, with care
cheertee, chiertee, love, charity
chees, chese, chose
cherice, cherish
cheuissance, achievement
cheuyce, provide, achieve
childissch, childly, immature, inexperienced
chyldhode, inexperience
chynchy, niggardly
chynes, chynnyng, chink(s), gap(s)
chyste, money chest
clappe, chatter; **clappyd,** chattered
clept, called
clernesse, brightness
cleued, clung; **cleueth,** clings
clippe, embrace
cloos, stronghold
cloos, close, shut
cloudeful, impure, clouded
cofre, coffer, money chest
cofred, put into a money chest
colde, turn cold; **coldith,** chills
colours, rhetorical and stylistic devices
combreworld, person who encumbers life
compaine, compaignie, company
compleyne, complaint
conceit, conceyt, idea, belief
conioyned, conjoined, linked
conquere, gain, regain
conseil, secret
conseil, consail, advice

contrarie, oppose, be at variance with
conueniently, aptly
conuertible, of one kind
coost, region, country
cote, coat
cotidian, daily
countinaunce, countenance
countrefete, imitate, feign
coupable, blameworthy
couyne, deception
cowde, cowden, could
crabbidnesse, harshness
craftily, skilfully
crauour, beggar
cure, care
custume, habit, usage
custumed, accustomed

daliaunce, conversation
dalt, distributed
dampnable, damned
daswed, dazed
daunger, enforcement
debate, strive
debonaire, gracious
dedly, fearful, mortal
dcede, dead, hidden
deel, del, part
deep, muddy (way)
deffendynge, forbidding
delauee, dissolute
deliure, deliver
deme, think, judge; **demed,** thought; **demeth,** thinks
demene, demean
depraue, slander
dere, harm, injure
derlyng, favourite, darling
desdeyn, disdain
deskeuere, reveal
despende, spend
despenses, spending, expenditure
despent, shed, spent
despitous, pitiful
desport, desporten, dysporte, play, amuse oneself, entertain
desteyned, slandered
dettour, debtor
dewynge, bedewing
deyneth, deigns; **deynen,** deign
deyntee, choice piece
diffende, preserve

dileccioun, love, affection
dirke, dark
dirknesse, darkness
displesaunt, unpleasing
disport, sport, play
dissert, merit, dessert
disseuerance, separation
disseuere, separate
disshed, dispersed, wasted
distaunce, disdain, pride
doel, grief
dote, meddle
doun right, absolutely
dou3tre, daughter
drecche, injure, slander
dreede, fear, doubt
drempt, dreamed
drery, joyless
dresse, dressen, go (refl.), prepare;
   dressid, prepared
dryen, suffer, endure
dryueth, makes its way, put
   (aside)
dyuyne, contrive, devise

echon, each one
edifie, build, increase
eelde, age
eft, again
egal, equal
eiled, ailed
eischewyt, avoids
eke, also
elles, else
emperice, empress
emprise, empryse, undertaking
enable, make able
enchantours, magicians
enchesoun, reason
encomborus, distressing
encombrid, tangled, dismayed
endyte, write, compose
endytyng, composition
enfourmeth, informs
enlumyne, illuminate
ensaumple, example
ensaumpleth, take as an example
enspire, inspire
entaill, engraving
entaill, engrave
entendement, understanding
entremete, meddle
enuenemous, poisonous

enuolupid, enveloped
eny, any
equypolent, equivalent
eres, ears
ernestful, important, serious
erst, before
eschew, esche, eschue, escape,
   avoid(ed)
esid, eased
estat, condition, circumstance
esy, easy
exaudicioun, praying aloud
excite, incite, inspire
excusacion, excuse
execut, put in hand, done
ey, alas
eyle, ail, harm

fader, fadir, father
faille, fail; faylyng, lacking, failing;
   faylyth, fails; it is no faille,
   sans faille, without any doubt
fare, happening, matter
farsid, stuffed
fauel, flattery, flatterer
feeld, felt
feendly, wicked
feere, companion; in fere, to-
   gether
fel, fell, shrewd, cunning
fele, many
fer, for
ferd, afraid
ferden, fared
ferdful, fearful
ferfoorth, far
fern ago, long ago; ferne yeer,
   last year
fers, fierce
feruence, zeal
feruent, burning, zealous
fette, fetched
feyned, feynt, feigned, faint
feyntyd, caused to lose heart
feynter, smoother, softer
feyntere, assuager, reliever
ficche, fix; ficchid, fixed
fikilnesse, fickleness
fil, fyl, fell, befell
filwedist, followed
flytte, fly, separate
flyttyng, unstable
foleye, commit a folly

folie, folly
foltisshe, foolish
folwe, follow; folwed, followed; folwith, follows
folwere, followers
fool, foolish
force, matter, importance
foreward, promise
forthoghte, repented
forthy, therefore
forueye, stray
foryeue, forgive; foryued, forgave
foryeuenesse, forgiveness
foryite, forget
fostred, fostered
fourmeel, regularly trained
fownden, found; fowndid, established
foysoun, plenty
free, generous
freined, asked
fretynge, biting, worrying
fructuous, fruitful
fyn, end

gapyd, longed for
gastnesse, fear
gelous, jealous
gere, matter
gerynesse, fickleness
girt, pierced
gleede, coal
glistren, glisten, shine
glose, explanation, telling
glose, explain, tell
glosyngly, spaciously
good, property
goostly, spiritual, in a spiritual manner
gore, gown
gouernaylle, control, management
grame, vexation
grame, vexatious
graueth, digs
grede, call, cry for
gree, acceptance
greeable, acceptable
greef, greeue, grief
greuance, grievance, harm
gripe, seize, comprehend
grope, find, search for
grot, groat
grownde, base, stand upon
gru, particle, grain

grucche, complain
guerdoun, reward
guyse, gyse, disguise
gye, lead, guide; gyeth, leads; gyded, guided

habownde, abound
hale, whole, sound
halkes, hiding-places
halt, holds
halte, walk, go
halwyd, hallowed
harwe, harrow
hastyf, speedy, swift
haunted, frequented
hawe, fruit of hawthorn
heep, crowd
heetith, promises
hele, heal
helid, covered
helþe, health
hem, them
hennes, hence
hent, took, seized
hernes, corners
herit, hears
hertyth, heartens, inspires
hethenesse, heathen land
heuy, sad, woeful, sorry
hie, hy, high
hie, hye, hieth, hasten
hight, hi3t, promised; on highte, in hope
hilded, poured
ho, stop
hold, fortress
holde, holden, beholden; preserve, believe
holsum, healthy
honestee, reputation
hoolly, wholly
hore, age, grow grey
hyly, highly
hyne, servant
hynes, highness
hyre, her, their

idel, empty, vain; an idel, in vain
ile, island
ilyche, alike
indigences, poverty
inly, alone with one's self
inned, reaped, gathered
inow, enough

inpotence, weakness
insipience, lack of knowledge, folly
i-ete, eaten
imaade, made
iment, intended
iseyd, said
iwrouȝt, made
iwys, indeed
iangle, chatter; iangeled, chattered
ieet, jet
iowes, jaws
ioynt, joint
iuge, judge
iust, just

kakele, cackle, gossip
keene, sharp
keep, notice
kepte, took care, intended
keuere, cover
kid, known
kirtil, shirt, gown
knouleche, knowledge
konneth thank, give thanks
konnyng, wisdom
kouthe, known
kowde, could
kus, kiss
kyst, kissed
kythe, kythist, make known

laborious, hard-working
labouren, belabour
lagh, dues, subscription
lak, censure
lappe, sleeve, fold; by the lappe, at hand
large, wide, generous; at his large, at his liberty
largeliche, widely
largesse, generosity, free-spending
lawghe, laugh, smile
lawhyng, smiling
leche, physician
leef, dear
leered, educated
lees, leese, lie
leesist, lose
leet, caused, did
leeued, believed
leke, leek
lene, slight
lenger, longer, more distant

lese, of less value
lese, lose
lesse, lesynge, lie
leste, least
lette, hinder
letterure, education
lettynge, restriction
leue, leave
leuer, rather
lewde, ignorant, lay
lewdenesse, ignorance
licken, liken; lickned, likened
lige, liege
ligeance, allegiance
lightlees, unenlightened
likerous, of large appetite
limitacioun, licence
list, likes, pleases (impers.)
lith, lies (in ambush)
liuere, livery
lode, load
logged, lodged, camped
lok, lock
loos, reputation, praise
loos, loose
lore, wisdom
lore, lorne, lest
losel, traitor
losengeour, flatterer
lucre, money
lust, will, pleasure,
lustyli, freely, with a goodwill
lyfly, with life
lyflynesse, freshness, clarity
lyflode, livelihood
lykith, pleases
lym, limb, arm
lyme, lime, the sticky lime used by fowlers
lyme, lime, ensnare
lyte, little
lyȝtly, easily

macche, equal
maistrie, maystry, a sovereign cure, a great task; for the maistrie, above all others
maistrieth, rules; maistried, ruled
marc, mark (i.e. 6s. 8d.)
marchandie, merchandise
martire, martyrdom
mate, overcome, checkmate
maugree, resentment

maugree, in spite of
mazidnesse, apathy, shame
mede, meadow
mediatrice, intercessor
meede, reward
meeued, affected, excited
mene, intercessor; the middle way
mene, poor, mean
mene, intend, mean; meneth, means
merciable, merciful
meruailled, wondered
meryer, more pleasant
meschef, myschef, harm, distress
mescreance, miscreance, heresy
messe, mass
messe, dine
mesure, quantity
mete, food
metrid, scanned
meue, move, advise
meynee, gathering, body of men
Mighelmesse, Michaelmas
mirie, miry, pleasant, joyful
miroure, reflect
mis, amiss, wrongly
misericorde, pity
misgyed, misled
mishappyd, deformed
misreule, unruly life
missettist, misplace
mochil, much, great
modir, mother
moisture, liquid
mone, complaint
mood, mind, thought, spirit
moot, must
mortified, withered
morwe, morning
moustre, show, make an appearance
mowe, may
mowled, stained
mowthe, mouth; hath in mouthe, has on one's lips
mynde, inclination, desire
myngith, reminds, suggests
mynystreth, tend, give heed to
myrith, bemires
mystook, forgot his duty, misbehaved (refl.)
myte, mite, fraction
my3tte, my3tten, might

namely, especially
narwe, narrow
nede, nedes, necessarily
neer, nearer
nere, we're not
nere, never
neuene, name
nightirtale, night time
nis, is not
nobles, noblis, nobles (the coins)
nobleye, nobility
nolde, would not
nones, time, occasion
norice, nurse
nort, naught
not, do not know
notise, warning
nowder, neither
nouelrie, novelty
nowder, neither
nou3t, no3t, not, naught
nusance, harm, power to harm
ny, nigh, almost
nyce, foolish
nycetee, folly, concern
nygon, niggard, miser

ooth, oath
opne, open
or, ere, before
orisoun, prayer
ornat, ornate, decorated
other, or
ouerlarge, over-liberal
out, owt, speak, utter
outrage, excess
outrageous, excessive
outrance, extremity, utter limits
outrayed, overcome, expelled
ou3te, owned
owter, speaker, one who utters
oynement, ointment, salve

pamfilet, small book
papeiay, parrot
par, per, by; par cas, by chance; par compagnie, for company's sake; pardee, by God; parfay, by faith
parcloos, partition, wall
parforned, performed
partie, part

passyngly, exceedingly
patente, letter patent, written royal command
pauyment, paved surface
pay, pleasure
peere, equal
peise, weigh; peisith, weighs
peisible, in peace, without dispute
pekkyd, pecked; pekkyd moode, became angry
pensyf, pensive
pentice, overhang, penthouse
perauenture, by chance
pere, pear
perueide, granted
pesecod, pea husk
peyne, exertion, activity
peynture, painting, picture
peys, weight, balance
pighte, pitched
piler, pillar
pistle, story
planed, erased
pleneer, full
plesaunce, pleasantry
plite, plight
plotmel, piece by piece
port, demeanour
pouert, poverty
powke, wicked man
preef, proof
prees, crowd, preparation, haste; putte in prees, exert oneself
preet, ready
prest, ready
preue, prove, test
priuee, secret, private
probacioun, experience, testing
profrid, offered
prow, benefit
pryme, early morning, about 9 a.m.
pryuee, privy, aware of
pryuetee, secrets
pullaylle, poultry
purchace, obtain
purueied, arranged
putte, impute
pyked, adorned, well prepared
pynchid, found fault with
payne, torment, pain

queynt, qweynt, quenched
quyte, qwyten, leave, requite;
quite, qwit, required, released, made free
qweeme, appease
qwenche, quench, overcome;
queynt, quenched
qwikne, inspire life, quicken
qwook, shook

rafte, reft
ragerie, horse-play, romp
rakil, hasty
rascaill, rabble
real, rial, royal
recche, rekke, reck, heed; rekkeþ, heeds
receite, receiver
reclus, recluse,
reconforten, entertain
recreacioun, regeneration
rede, advise; redde, advised
reed, counsel, advice
reek, smoke
reewe, rue
refreyned, caused to refrain, stopped
refuyt, refuge
regiment, regimen, rule
reioisan, rejoice
releeue, help, aid
remeynynge, remaining
rentes, income
repeir, company
repreef, reprove
repreuable, worthy of censure
rere, raise; rese, rose
resorte, go to, resort
retenance, retinue
reue, deprive
reuel, joy, celebration
reuled, ruled, amenable
reward, dessert
rietous, given to riot, difficult
riot, unruly living
riotours, dissolute young men
risshes, rushes, reeds
rolled, threw continuously about
roo, hind
rootid, deep-rooted
rowe, row, line; in þe rowe, in the company

rowne, whisper; rowned, whispered
rownyngly, quietly
russchynge, rushing
ryf, common, plentiful
ryfle, steal
rype, reap, cutdown

sad, sadde, serious, sober
sadde, become serious, decline
sadnesse, seriousness
saillen, sail; saillid, sailed
salewyng, greeting
salue, salve
salut, health, safety
sanz, without
saphir, saphire
sauf, except
saute, leap
sauter, psalter
sauuacioun, salvation
sawe, wisdom
scare, slight
schapen, contrive, intend; schapyþ, prepares; schoop, schope, shoop, happened, contrived, planned
science, knowledge
scripture, writing
secree, secret
seeke, sick
seelde, seelden, seldom
segh, say, sy, sygh, saw
sei, seist, say, sayest; seidest, said
seisyne, legal title
sely, naïve, innocent
semblable, similar
sentence, wisdom
seruage, servitude
seruiture, service
sese, seize
sesonynge, seasoning
setten by, lay aside, disregard
seur, safe, certain
seuretee, seurtee, safety
seurly, safely
shadde, shed
shadwe, shadwist, shadow
shamefast, shy, awkward
shamely, modest, abashed
shape, befell (refl.), shapith, intends
shent, shamed, punished
shilde, prevent, shield
shit, shut

shone, shun
shoo, shoe
shoon, shone
shour, confict, attack, shower
shuln, shall
sikir, syker, sure, safe
sikirnesse, sykernesse, safety
sit, befits
site, cite
sith, sithin, since
siȝynge, sighing
skile, reason
slaghtree, slaughter
sleeth, slays
slipir, slyper, slippery, untrustworthy
slow, slough
slow, killed
sly, cunning, deliberate
smert, wound, harm, grief
smothee, closely
socour, help
solempnely, ceremonially
solempnitee, ceremony
somme, sum
song, sang
soothe, truth
soothfastnesse, truthfulness, truth
soothly, truly
sore, grievously, sorely
sorrer, more sorely
sotil, subtle, clever
sotiltee, subtlety, cleverness
souffissance, ability
souffraunce, patience
soule, alone, sole
soun, sound
soustenour, upholder
sowe, sown
sowke, sowken, suck, suckle
sowneth, pertains to
soyle, satisfy, answer
spaak, spak, spoke
specialtee, particular favour, distinction
spectacle, pair of spectacles
speede, prosper; sped, satisfied
speek, speak
spilte, spylt, broken
stage, platform, height
stak, was fastened
stalle, place, lodge
stant, stands
steerne, stern

steruen, die
stide, place, stead
stif, unyilding
stikith, sticks, strikes
stirynge, inciting, inspiring
stoor, store
streit, straight, closely confined
streynynge, strain
stuf, matter
stynte, stop; styntith, stops
styre, stir, advise; stired, incited
sue, follow
suppoaille, support, aid
swal, swelled
swich, such
swoot, sweat, perspiration
sy, sygh, saw
symple, unlearned, humble
symplesse, lowness of estate
syn, synt, sythe, since
synguleer, limited to one

taar, tore, rent
taille, score, reckoning
tak, take, give, receive, take
talent, appetite, desire
tapyt, cloth
telle, count; tolde, set store by
tete, breast, teat
thank, gratitude due to someone; his thankes, with his consent, willingly
the, thee
the, prosper
thirle, pierce
tho, then
threst, thriste, thrust
thrid, third
thristy, thirsty
throwe, time
thrystyth, desires; thrystynge, desiring
thynkith me, it seems to me
thys, this, this man
to and to, completely
tofore, toforn, before
tor, torent, rent
tourn, turn, legal circuit
trauaille, work
trauayllous, arduous
tretyce, treatise
triacle, remedy
trussid, departed, went off (*refl.*)

tryce, thrust
tunge, tongue
tweye, two
tweynne, twynne, depart, separate; twynned, departed
tyde, befall
tyde, time, hour

þinke, think
þouȝte, thought, anxiety
þouȝtful, full of thought or anxiety

vnbuxum, unwilling
vncofred, took from chest
vndeffouled, immaculate
vnethe, vnnethe, scarcely, with difficulty
vnfeyned, frank
vnkeuered, uncovered
vnkunnyng, ignorance
vnkunnyng, ignorant
vnlust, disinclination
vnmeeble, unmovable (of goods)
vnpike, pick (a lock)
vprightes, justly, straightforwardly
vnsad, light-headed
vnschyt, unshut, open
vnseur, uncertain
vnsikirnesse, danger, uncertainty
vnsyghte, lack of slight
vnsyker, uncertain
vnwar, unknown, unaware
vnwist, unknown

vengeable, vengeful
venym, poison
verraily, truly
verray, verre, true, real
vertu, virtue, moral law, power
viage, expedition, pilgrimage
voide, absent oneself, put out, go out

waar, careful
wacche, keep awake
wach, wakefulness
wafres, cakes
walwyd, turned restlessly
wardeyn, keeper
warie, wary
warned, advised, given notice

waue, draw, move; **wauynge**, moving
wawes, waves
waymentynge lamentation
wedde, pledge, pawn
weene, wene, think, expect; **weeneth**, thinks
weldy, fit
wele, well-being
weleful, full of joy or well-being
welthe, welþe, wealth, benefit
wemmelees, spotless
wepne, weapon
were, wear; **werith**, wears
wern, were
werne, deny, refuse
werre, war
werre, worse
werreye, harnass, harry; **werreyeth**, harries
werreyour, warrior, enemy
werse, worse
wexe, increase
weye, weigh
weyke, weak
weuye, avoid; **weyued**, removed
wight, wyth, wyȝt, man
wighte, weight
wiis, wise
wirkynge, wyrkyng, action
wist, wyst, known
wit, wyt, intelligence, sign of wisdom, judgement
wite, learn, know
wold, power
wond, wont, accustomed
wondir, exceptionally
wone, dwell
wone, custom, amount
woo bistaad, beset by woe
wood, mad

woodnesse, madness
woot, knows; **wost, woost**, knowest; **wostow**, knowest thou
worsship, honour, reputation
wowed, wooed
wrake, sin, evil
wrecche, wretch; wretched
wreke, punish, revenge
wrenches, breakings, violations
wrythed, struggled
wyly, cunning

yaf, gave
yald, yielded
yate, gate
ye, yen, eye(s)
yerned, yearn
yeue, yeuen, give; **yeuest**, gives; yaf, gave; **youe, youen**, given
yifte, gift
yilde, requite; **yildinge**, yielding
ympe, son, offspring
ynnynge, reaping, stacking
yore, formerly
youe, youen, given

ybent, bowed
ymeeued, advised, moved
yrootid, rooted

ȝate, gate
ȝeerly, yearly
ȝelde, requite; ȝyldeth, yields
ȝelowenesse, yellowness
ȝeme, care, attention
ȝong, young
ȝore, formerly, long ago
ȝour, your
ȝoures, yours
ȝyde, went
ȝysterday, yesterday